W9-BSB-370

The Edge of Madness

ROBERT A. LISTON

THE EDGE

Prisons and

OF MADNESS

Prison Reform in America

Franklin Watts, Inc., New York • 1972

The author and publisher wish to thank the following for permission to reprint from works for which they own the copyrights.

The Federal Penitentiary, Atlanta, Georgia, for excerpts from the *Atlantian* magazine, which appear on pp. 67–68.

The New York Times, for excerpts that appear on pp. 56–60, 65–67 from the *New York Times Magazine:* "A Judge is a Con, A Con is a Judge" by Richard Hammer, 9/14/69, and on pp. 91–92 from "Rikers—The City's Island of the Damned" by Harvey Swados, 4/26/70. Copyright © 1969/1970 by The New York Times Company. Reprinted by permission.

Pathfinder Press, Inc., for excerpts that appear on pp. 42–43, 61–64, 69–70 from *Black Voices from Prison* by Etheridge Knight. Reprinted by permission of Pathfinder Press, Inc. Copyright © 1970 by Pathfinder Press, Inc.

The Viking Press, Inc., for excerpts that appear on pp. 37, 96, 116–117 from *The Crime of Punishment* by Karl Menninger, M.D. Copyright © 1966, 1968 by Karl Menninger, M.D. All rights reserved. Reprinted by permission of The Viking Press, Inc.

To Clyde and Margie Newstrand

Contents

PART II **The Solutions**

Introduction

There is an instant problem in writing about prisons and prison reform. It is not really possible to discuss the subject without also discussing the police and the courts, for the nation's jails and prisons receive the products of both of these institutions. The result is likely to be a book on "crime in America." I have tried to describe the roles of the police and the courts in the corrections system, while focusing on the problems of the prisons and of the men and women in them. I have also tried to approach the problem rationally and factually, for I am convinced that emotionalism and sensationalism bar our goal of prison reform.

I have made use of and cite my own experiences as a

newspaperman and magazine journalist but I am indebted to
the following people who helped with the research: Claudia
Cohl, my editor; my good friend Clyde F. Newstrand; Jeff
Wallin, a senior student, and Thelma Bumbaugh, librarian
at Hiram College, who together made pertinent books available to me; and to Eleanor R. Seagraves, a resident of Washington, D. C., who unearthed many excellent and little-known
sources of information in the nation's capital.

R.A.L.
Benalmadena Costa, Spain
July 1971

PART I The Problem

1 A Self-Defeating System

On September 9, 1971, more than one thousand inmates of the New York State prison at Attica, near Buffalo, rioted. They seized more than thirty prison guards as hostages and barricaded themselves into a large wing of the institution.

What followed was an American tragedy.

Although four separate investigations of the matter were launched almost immediately after the incidents, many details are still shrouded in confusion. The essential facts seem to be these. Attica prison held twenty-two hundred inmates, of whom 85 percent were blacks and Puerto Ricans. The inmates had long complained about poor food, inadequate water, and infestations of flies. Racial tensions were at the breaking point between the inmates and their guards, all of whom were white.

Only a spark was needed to set off the riot. It came when guards beat a prisoner and threw him into solitary confinement. At breakfast, first an order to line up and march off was ignored, then the riot erupted. Fights broke out. Fires were set. Within minutes the guards were rounded up and held as hostages. Prisoners armed themselves with knives, spears, clubs, and other homemade weapons. In reaction to this move, other guards, state troopers, and eventually national guardsmen rushed to the prison. A major confrontation was created.

From behind their barricades the inmates, about five hundred of whom were allegedly actively involved, issued a series of demands. They wanted better food and living conditions; payment of the state minimum wage for work in prison industries; "religious freedom"; the firing or transferring of the prison warden; employment of guards and prison officials from minority groups; creation of an "ombudsman" to handle inmate grievances; and full amnesty, or pardon, for any crimes committed by inmates during the rioting. They also wanted a group of citizens known to be sympathetic to the problems of minority groups and prisoners brought in as "observers" during negotiations. Finally, they wanted Governor Nelson A. Rockefeller to come to Attica personally to negotiate the issues.

Governor Rockefeller refused, stating his belief that he could accomplish nothing. State Commissioner of Correction Russell G. Oswald eventually assented to all the inmate demands but one. He and the governor insisted they had no legal authority to grant the amnesty from prosecution, particularly when a guard died after either being thrown or falling from the besieged building. A large question remains unanswered: Why did it take a full-scale riot and confrontation before state prison officials would agree to provide such things as better food, payment of legal minimum wages, ombudsmen, and more black guards? Why hadn't these fundamentals been provided in the first place?

Lines hardened over the demand for amnesty. Ultimatums were issued. One of the observers, United States Representative Herman Badillo of New York, a Puerto Rican, urged the governor, Oswald, and all concerned to "spend time and not lives" in solving the dispute. Another mediator, attorney William Kunstler, urged state officials to learn "patience" as a "virtue" even if the confrontation went on for six months.

In the end, Mr. Oswald ordered seventeen hundred state troopers and national guardsmen to storm the prison. Using helicopters, which dumped "tons of tear gas," and firing shotguns, rifles, and pistols, the uniformed men forced their way into the prison and ended the riot. In the melee ten hostages and thirty-two inmates were killed. More than a hundred others were seriously injured. The death toll was expected to rise. Initial word was that the hostages died because their throats had been slashed by the prisoners. Medical examiners later found this was not so. Guards had been killed by gunshot wounds, some with as many as a dozen bullets in them. When no guns were found among the prisoners' weapons, it was concluded that the hostages had all died in the gunfire from the troopers and national guardsmen.

A monstrous tragedy, certainly. Forty-two dead. For what?

The "incident" at Attica followed by less than two weeks

a series of deaths at San Quentin prison in California, which was generally considered to be among the best and most progressive prisons in the United States. As in Attica, the truth is hidden by confusion and conflicting information. But the essential facts seem to be that George Jackson, author of *Soledad Brother: The Prison Letters of George Jackson,* either had a gun or obtained one from a visitor who smuggled it in to him. In a melee, described by authorities as an attempted prison break, Jackson was killed by gunfire from prison guards as he allegedly fled across a prison yard. Three guards and two white inmates were also killed, either with guns or with knives. The truth of what really happened remains to be discovered. Those sympathetic to Jackson charge that he was "set up" and "cut down" by prison officials. Certainly a man who was much admired for his literary style and his revolutionary zeal was dead.

There are many questions and problems raised by the deaths at Attica and San Quentin, all of which are discussed in the pages to come. At the moment we may say four things about these two very recent, very tragic incidents.

Futile. Self-defeating. Wasteful. Disgraceful.

These words describe the American prison system as a whole. They have been used by presidents, governors, members of innumerable investigative commissions, social scientists, and administrators of prisons for at least a century.

Futile. The entire purpose of prisons is to prevent people from committing crimes—either by keeping them locked up so they *cannot* or by reforming them so they *will not*. The American prison system fails abysmally on both counts.

On any given day about half a million American men, women, and juveniles are behind bars. We read in a newspaper that an offender has been given a five- or ten- or twenty-year sentence and feel safer because he is in prison. But when this person enters prison, another is released, having served that five-, ten-, or twenty-year sentence.

Are the nineteen out of twenty prisoners who return to society reformed? Do they take a productive place in that society? In an appeal for prison reform, President Richard M. Nixon gave this reply:

In some instances, the answer is yes. But in an appalling number of cases, our correctional institutions are failing. According to recent studies, some forty per cent of those who are released from confinement later return to prison. Or, to put it another way, a sizeable proportion of serious crimes are committed by persons who have already served a jail sentence. Eight out of every ten offenders sampled in a recent FBI study had at least one prior arrest and seven out of ten had a prior conviction. Of those charged with burglary, auto theft or armed robbery, between sixty and seventy per cent had been arrested two or more times in the preceding seven years.

For youthful offenders, the picture is even darker. The repeater rates are greater among persons under twenty than over [that age]. . . .

In addition to the estimated 40 percent of the exconvicts who return to prison, perhaps *another* 40 percent commit crimes that go undetected.

President Nixon called this "a record of . . . futility."

Self-defeating. Jails and prisons *increase,* not decrease crime. ". . . there is evidence," said the president, "that our institutions actually compound crime problems by bringing young delinquents into contact with experienced criminals."

Our jails and prisons are literally schools of crime. During an interview with a seventeen-year-old reformatory inmate who had stolen more than fifty bicycles, I asked him what he had learned in prison. "I learned how to crack safes," he said.

Perhaps even worse than such "lessons" is the release of convicts who are embittered, untrained, and totally ill-equipped to cope with the life conditions that led them to crime in the first place. They are distrusted by society and forced into a life of unemployment or menial labor, which encourages them to turn again to crime.

Wasteful. The United States has about four hundred federal and state prisons, penitentiaries, reformatories, farms, training schools, and other "correctional" institutions. There are about four thousand local jails and unknown thousands of lockups where people are held for hours or days. A great deal of money is needed to operate all these facilities. Americans spend about one and a half *billion* dollars a year on something that only worsens the problem it is intended to solve. It costs an estimated $11,000 a year to keep one family man in prison, including both the cost of his incarceration and that of keeping his family on welfare while he is behind bars.

All this is certainly disgraceful.

The American system of "corrections"—a misnomer if there ever was one—has been denounced by literally everyone involved with it or knowledgeable about it. American corrections has *no* defenders.

Consider the words of Richard Hughes, former governor of New Jersey, who is chairman of the American Bar Association's Council on Correctional Reform.

He called our corrections system a "frightening national disaster" that contributes to the "phenomenon of mounting crime and brutality, wasting untold sums of money, and despoiling successive generations of youth which might otherwise be saved."

He called his task with the American Bar Association "an opportunity to assist in cleaning up a confused morass which inflicts great present harm and poses a very frightening eminent threat to American society."

Then he quoted a judge as saying; "I not only have to hold my nose, I have to anesthetize my conscience to send men to the Department of Corrections."

Chief Justice Warren E. Burger of the Supreme Court has said, "Without effective correctional systems an increasing proportion of our population will become chronic criminals with no other way of life except the revolving door of crime, prison and more crime."

Richard W. Velde, associate administrator of the Law Enforcement Assistance Administration, a United States Government agency established to begin the task of correctional reform, told a Senate subcommittee, "The conditions of the jails and institutions of this country constitutes one of the most despicable of the nation's social disgraces."

He said the problem was "beyond the capabilities" of states and localities to solve.

Then there is the statement of Negley K. Teeters, a college professor, in the publication *Federal Probation:*

Indeed, the prison presents an abysmal graveyard of blighted expectations which shows little promise of improvement despite the heroics of correctional personnel, enlightened lay citizens, understanding legislators and organizations and societies dedicated to reform. . . . The whole system is corrosive and totally unworthy of our best motives and capabilities. It is almost hopelessly bogged down, creaking, outmoded and confusing in both its philosophy and its operation.

Such quotes denouncing the American prison system could go on until they filled this book. Hardly anyone thinks the system has any merit or finds anything about it to commend.

America's prison problem and the need for reform has great immediacy. Recent opinion polls have shown that the national problem of "crime in the streets" is a major concern of Americans. Yet, people who fear and lament the murders, rapes, assaults, and muggings in the streets, who are victims of the robberies, burglaries, and thefts of their property, seldom give a second thought to the prisons that "manufacture" the criminals who commit those crimes.

When Governor Hughes and Velde made the statements already quoted, they were addressing the Subcommittee on National Penitentiaries of the Senate Committee on the Judiciary. Listening to them was one man, Senator Quentin N. Burdick of North Dakota. The other four senators on the subcommittee did not even bother to attend the session.

Yet, Americans "know" or think they know about prisons. Life behind bars is a common theme of books, movies, and television shows. Several times a year newspapers, magazines, and television news programs spotlight the problem for a day or two, but then the light goes out and prisons go on largely as before.

The publicity usually takes the form of one of two types of "horror stories"—those about crimes committed by former prisoners and those about the brutal treatment of prisoners. Both are easily illustrated.

In August 1969, a number of individuals entered the Los Angeles home of movie actress Sharon Tate, who was eight months pregnant at the time. She and three of her friends were tortured and then brutally and grotesquely murdered, their bodies mutilated. Steven Parent, an eighteen-year-old bystander, was murdered in front of the house. The following night, wealthy grocer Leon La Bianca and his wife were killed in a similar fashion in their nearby home. After investigation, police arrested a man named Charles Manson and three young women. They were charged and convicted of murder after an eight-month trial.

There were undoubtedly many influences in the life of Charles Manson, but he is most definitely a product of the American corrections system. He spent time in various institutions for juveniles and served jail and penitentiary sentences for car theft, forgery, and other crimes, including a seven-year "stretch" in prison in the state of Washington.

The California jury that convicted Manson and his female companions sought to relieve the American prison system of the responsibility for reforming them. After prolonged deliberations, the jury ordered him and the women executed. His conviction and sentence are now being appealed to higher courts. As we shall see, the use of the death sentence is creating other, perhaps more horrendous problems than the prisons.

Tens of thousands, indeed, hundreds of thousands of similar stories could be told. Exconvicts, products of the American system of corrections, *do* commit crimes, horrible crimes, murders, robberies, rapes, assaults. They *do* truly *prey* on American citizens.

But lurid tales of crimes by exprisoners only worsen the problems of our prisons. The stories lead to public hysteria, encourage those who would "get tough" with criminals and would "lock them up and throw away the key," abandoning all efforts at rehabilitation. In the wake of the Manson trial, some juries began dispensing sentences as long as five hundred years—and one day. Because persons sentenced to "life" in prison can sometimes be released after as little as eight years, the jurors sought to keep the offenders in prisons by sentencing them to multiple lifetimes.

Rather than contributing to prison reform, get-tough attitudes cause much of the prison problem that exists. Many Americans are deluded by the notion that severe punishment is a deterrent to crime; that is, if a person knows that he will have to go to prison for many years and that prisons are awful places, he will not commit crimes. The simple facts are, however, that prisons *are* awful, men and women *are* sentenced to them for many years, yet the crime rate is *increasing*.

The second variety of publicity can only be described as "horror stories" about prison life and the mistreatment of prisoners.

An example is the Cummins Prison Farm in Arkansas, where two hundred convicts work sixteen thousand acres of cotton fields in what amounts to human slavery. They toil twelve hours a day without pay, supervised by men bearing shotguns and rifles. These armed men are the toughest of the convicts, murderers, and rapists. Cummins prisoners survive by selling their blood or their bodies. Drug addiction is rampant, along with gambling and loan sharking; stabbings, assaults, and rapes are common. One inmate, speaking of the fear that exists said, "There's no protection for your life. I keep thinking *if* I get out—not *when*."

Another example is an incident that took place in Illinois in the late 1960's. A woman involved in a complicated inheritance suit had defied a court order to let bank officials assess her home and was sentenced to a week in the Cook County Jail in Chicago for contempt of court. At the jail, she was ordered to disrobe, and her private parts were examined with unsterile instruments, presumably to see if she was concealing narcotics. She was put in an enclosure with sixty-eight other women, given dirty linen, and thrust into a cell infested with bedbugs. During her week in jail, she discovered women walked around barebreasted in front of male guards; new prisoners were sexually assaulted in the showers by other women; and the toilets were used for smuggling narcotics. She saw an obviously disturbed woman being driven to the point of self-destruction by the taunts of other prisoners. The well-to-do, highly respected woman was badly burned when scalding water was thrown on her during a fight between two other prisoners, but she received no medical treatment.

Such tales have a certain usefulness in that when published, these stories about jails and prisons where inmates are treated brutally lead to reforms. The Cook County Jail was improved. A federal judge has ordered the Cummins Farm either to be reformed or closed down. Nearly all prisons have abandoned such brutal practices as thrusting prisoners into solitary confinement in "the hole," and sadistic guards have been fired or severely restricted in their actions.

The difficulty with horror stories as illustrations of the prison problem is that such extreme conditions are not the norm. Most prisoners receive at least adequate food, clothing, and shelter, and relatively few are beaten or brutalized. Virtually all wardens and other prison officials are not sadists, but are knowledgeable, experienced, dedicated, sometimes inspired men who are endeavoring to accomplish a nearly hopeless task with very limited resources. As one of them, Dr. E. Preston Sharp, General Secretary of the American Correctional Association, put it, "Rather than have the so-called bizarre exposés do what some of the so-called sincere people state, of getting people roused to assist in improving corrections, it is having a negative effect on the other side."

The horror stories also serve to detract from the real problem, which is that most prisoners only serve time. Almost nothing is done to rehabilitate them, and what is done frequently does not work. Worse, prison administrators are far from certain which programs are truly effective in rehabilitating prisoners.

Lurid tales contribute only to the emotionalism that surrounds the entire problem of crime and punishment in the United States—for the emotions conflict. At the same time, Americans want to get tough with criminals and to stop brutalizing them so they can be reformed. The "get-toughers" denounce the "bleeding hearts" who would "coddle" prisoners. Such words as "brutal" and "sadistic" are hurled in reply. Clearly, these emotional attitudes will just never be reconciled.

What is needed is less emotionalism and a more hardheaded, logical, practical approach to the problems of crime, prisons, and punishment. We need to recognize the futility, self-defeatism, and waste of our present system of corrections and to concentrate on seeking a more useful system. We need to examine the causes of crime and to find the best means of alleviating them.

These goals are hampered by the fact that not very much is known about the American corrections system. In part, this lack of information exists because the system is so thoroughly complicated. There is a federal prison system operated by the United States government. It is considered the best in the nation, for it strives to be a model for the fifty states, each of which operates its own prison system, consisting of penitentiaries (the infamous "pen"), reformatories, farms, training schools, and other institutions. In all states but two (Connecticut and Delaware), jails and other places of detention are maintained by city, county, township, and other local governments.

The result is a hodgepodge of institutions, ranging from a few that are "model," to some that are abysmal. Twenty-five prisons were built before the Civil War. As Governor Hughes pointed out:

The State Prison of New Jersey was originally opened in 1798 and was substantially rebuilt in 1836. Even now it has one wing containing cells in which four men are caged in a space originally designed for one. But even prisons constructed more recently are no better in design or programs or effectiveness.

The corrections system also includes a vast system of parole and probation, which again operates at the federal, state, and local levels.

The parole system is intended to be a means by which those convicts who have been "reformed" in prison can be identified and released. They are supposed to be supervised by a "parole officer" who observes their conduct and helps them lead a crime-free life. The power to decide who gets paroled is vested in a "parole board," a group of prominent citizens who examine the inmate's record and question him about his attitudes.

Probation is a system similar to parole. Instead of being sent to jail, an offender is placed under the supervision of a probation officer, who is supposed to prescribe rules governing the conduct of the offender, as well as see that he obeys those rules. At the very least, the offender is expected to meet periodically with his probation officer and to report on his employment, schooling, and other activities.

In addition, "probation officers" are called upon to provide information to federal, state, and local judges that will assist them in sentencing convicted offenders. A "presentence" report from the probation department includes information about the offender's background, family life, social conditions, and education, as well as opinions about his intelligence, attitudes, and potential for reform. On the basis of this report, the judge decides the nature of the sentence. He may use it in determining whether to sentence the offender to a penitentiary, reformatory, training school, or other institution and for how long. The report may also influence the judge to put the offender on probation.

Both parole and probation are forms of punishment in that they restrict the offender and his activities. At any given moment, acting on his own or on the recommendation of a parole or probation officer, a judge can take away the person's freedom and sentence him to prison as a parole or probation violator.

This, then, is the American system of corrections: imprisonment, parole, and probation, administered at multiple levels of government. The system also functions differently according to the age of the offender. Those persons under age sixteen or eighteen, depending upon local laws, are handled in juvenile courts. Those older are processed in various forms of adult courts.

This corrections system was worked out over hundreds of years, often haphazardly, but sometimes through thoughtful effort. Waves of reformers have left their mark upon the system, for good and ill. As we shall see, the system as it exists today is an amalgam of all those efforts at reform.

The first observation to make about the corrections system is its diversity. Its effectiveness varies from state to state, city to city—and even judge to judge. It embraces over 135,000 full- and part-time employees, wardens, guards, doctors, psychologists, sociologists, clergymen, parole and probation officers, and many more. These people range from intelligent and inspired to stupid and corrupt. But we move closer to understanding the prison problem if we acknowledge that they are all overworked. Each year an estimated 2.5 million people pass through the corrections system. At any given moment 1.3 million men, women, and juveniles are imprisoned or supervised by the corrections system. One-third are behind bars; two-thirds are on parole or probation.

The corrections system works an unknown percentage of time. Read *My Shadow Ran Fast* by Bill Sands or the *Autobiography of Malcolm X* to become familiar with the stories of just two exconvicts who were reformed. A night in jail, the assistance of a skilled probation officer have helped untold thousands of misguided youths to lead a normal life.

But, in sum, the corrections system fails to prevent or deter crime or to help the majority of people who come under its control. It fails abysmally, horribly, dreadfully. Why does it fail?

2 Getting into Prison

How does a person get into prison? Most Americans would declare that a simple question. He breaks the law, is arrested by police, convicted in court, and sentenced by a judge. Actually, the process is much more complicated than that. For most Americans, it is rather difficult to go to jail and extraordinarily hard to reach prison. It is somewhat "easier" if a person is poor, black, semi-literate, confused, mentally aberrated, misguided, and unlucky, but even that person has to "work at" going to prison.

The process of going to jail and/or prison is of crucial importance in understanding the problems of the American system of corrections and what is needed to reform it. The process involves crime, the police, and the courts, all of which are intricately involved with this system. They form the American System of Criminal Justice. How it functions intimately affects the person in jail or prison and his chances for reform.

Crime

Imprisonment is the principal method by which Americans (and most people of the world) seek both to punish and to reform wrong-doers. In the United States there are hundreds of crimes that call for imprisonment, including drunkenness; drug addiction; traffic offenses; myriad types of theft; fraud; and violent crimes, such as assault and murder.

These crimes are divided into three types: misdemeanors, felonies, and capital crimes. A misdemeanor is a minor offense that causes only inconvenience to society. Examples are drunkenness, disorderly conduct, small or petty thefts, trespassing on private property, loitering in a public place. There are scores of misdemeanors, any of which can lead to a jail sentence upon conviction. The term in jail can be as short as a day or a week, or as long as three years. A fine of money is a frequent punishment for a misdemeanor, but if the person cannot or will not pay the fine, he can be ordered to "work it off" in jail at the rate of a dollar or two a day. The legendary sentence for drunkenness or disorderly conduct is "thirty dollars or thirty days."

A felony is a more serious crime, and includes such offenses as burglary, theft of valuable property, armed robbery, serious assault, rape, and murder. The penalties for such crimes vary from state to state, but all call for more than one year in prison. Burglary might bring a sentence of five years; armed robbery, ten years; murder, life. All convicted felons are sentenced to state or federal prisons.

A capital crime, which calls for the death penalty, generally covers premeditated murder and, occasionally, rape. If the person is not sentenced to death, he is usually sent to prison for life.

These distinctions and penalties are prescribed by laws that were duly enacted by the representatives of the people. But the laws make many fine distinctions that seriously affect the person in jail or prison. If you force your way into your neighbor's home, you could be convicted of any of a variety of crimes, depending upon the circumstances and the attitudes of the police and prosecutor. You could be convicted of trespassing or illegal entry, both of which are misdemeanors. Or, you could be convicted of breaking and entering which, at worst, is a minor felony. If property is missing from the home, you could be convicted of burglary or of receiving stolen goods (a less serious crime). The severity of the sentence for burglary would depend upon the value of the goods stolen. If you committed the burglary in daylight, a lesser sentence would be called for than if you committed it at night. If persons were present in the home, you could be convicted of unarmed robbery. If you carried a weapon, the charge could be armed robbery.

The point is that there are people in prison serving widely different sentences for essentially the same crime. One may be in prison, a convicted felon, serving half his life. Another may be in for five years, a third in jail for six months, and a fourth may be walking the streets with a suspended sentence and probation.

These inconsistencies vitally affect the man behind bars. He may be embittered by the severity of his sentence compared to that of another man. He can easily tell himself, during those long years behind bars, that if he had been a little smarter, or had had a better lawyer to defend him, or had encountered a more lenient judge, that he, too, would have "gotten off" easier.

There is no fact of greater importance in understanding the prison problem that this: most crime in the United States is undetected, unreported, or unsolved.

Every second of every day undetected crimes are committed that could lead to imprisonment, some by criminals, others by "law-abiding" citizens. A man has too much to drink and drives his car; an executive pads his expense account; a taxpayer cheats on his income tax; a shopper steals a pair of stockings or a shirt; a storekeeper puts his fingers on the scales; a sportsman places an illegal bet; a smoker lights up some marijuana; an employee steals tools or materials from his employer; an adult offers a drink to a teenager; a person knowingly writes a bad check, planning to cover it in time. No one notices the crime. It occurs in secret, unobserved. It is labeled a "mistake," an "inevitable loss," "normal wear and tear." Perhaps only the saints have never committed crimes. We justify, we explain, but we are all guilty. No one knows this better than the man behind bars. He asks, "Why me?"

A large, but unknown percentage (some estimates are as high as 90 percent!) of crimes are detected, but go unreported to police. The victim may be involved in criminal activity and does not want the police asking questions. He may want to avoid embarrassment and publicity; he may not want to be bothered; he may claim he hasn't time to prosecute; he may feel it would not do any good to press charges for the police could never solve the crime.

Most crimes that are detected and reported are never solved by the police. The Federal Bureau of Investigation reports that nationwide only 20 percent of the crimes are "cleared," that is, the offender is identified and arrested. Police work hardest at solving violent crimes against persons. Anywhere from 56 to 85 percent of these crimes lead to arrests. But they are only a small percentage of the total number of crimes committed in the United States. The vast majority of crimes are against property and few are solved—only about 18 percent of the auto thefts and larcenies, 19 percent of the burglaries, and 27 percent of the robberies.

Can anyone wonder, considering all this, that the man sitting behind bars considers himself unlucky?

Police

The police of the United States are asked to do a nearly impossible task. They are expected to prevent crime, to detect that which takes place, and to arrest those who have done it. Moreover, they are to maintain order, be it among cars in rush hour or people demonstrating on behalf of civil rights, peace, or some other issue. They are, however, undermanned, underpaid, underequipped, and undertrained to accomplish such tasks. What is remarkable is not that they sometimes do the job so poorly, but that they sometimes do it so well.

Most police activities are beyond the scope of this book. The police functions that directly affect corrections are best shown by illustration.

Let us suppose you are standing on a street corner looking at a movie marquee, talking to a friend or simply minding your own business. Suddenly a squad car pulls up, the policemen inside jump out, inform you of your rights, demand that you identify yourself, frisk you for weapons, and arrest you. You are handcuffed and taken to the stationhouse. You ask what you did. You are told you stole a car.

It is unimportant to this discussion whether you actually did steal the car. What is important is that the police *think* you did. One witness saw you standing near the car, admiring it. Another person positively identified you as driving it. As auto theft cases go, the police think they have a pretty good one. You deny the crime. You admit you were standing near the car and, indeed, drove it. But you thought it belonged to a friend of yours, and when he offered to let you take a spin in it, you did. You had no idea it was stolen.

The police do not believe you. Yours is a most common story. In this heavily populated police district, several cars are stolen a night, hundreds in a year. The police want to do everything they can to stop the thefts. They question you about other recent thefts and accuse you of them, explaining "things will go easier for you" if you admit your guilt. When you refuse, saying you never stole any car, the detective shrugs and gives up. He has a lot of other, more important cases.

The police play a crucial role in corrections at this point, for they determine the charge against you. If they had time and were willing, they could investigate your alibi, arrest your friend, and release you. They could decide that the evidence against you only warrants a charge of receiving stolen goods or even the lesser charge of unauthorized use of other people's property. But no. They have two excellent witnesses to identify you. They wish to solve auto-theft cases, which are difficult to solve at best. You are charged with grand larceny—booked, fingerprinted, and placed in the jailhouse lockup, along with a few drunks, sex offenders, and others arrested that evening.

What happens to you next depends on one word—money. Let us suppose that you come from a middle-class home and that you know a little bit about your rights. When the police explain these rights to you—that anything you say can be held against you and that you have the right to remain silent and to call a lawyer—you insist that you be allowed to call your parents. Within a matter of minutes, your mother and father arrive, accompanied by a lawyer, who tells you to remain silent. He begins actions to have you released. You may spend the night in jail, but the following morning the lawyer has appeared before a judge and you are released on bail, that is, your family raises a sum of money in cash or by obtaining loans on property that ensures you will return for your trial. You go home, return to your job or school, and carry on a semblance of normal life.

Now let us suppose you are not so fortunate. You are so confused and frightened that you do not understand that you are permitted to make a phone call. Or, the phone call does no good. Your family is so poor that they have no possible way to hire an attorney or to raise the bail. The police will move you out of the stationhouse lockup into a van and transport you to the city jail. There you will be "processed," which consists of being stripped, searched, and examined. You will be given a uniform and put in a cell to await your appearance in court. If your family remains unable to raise the bail money and you continue to insist upon your innocence, you run a great risk of spending months in jail simply awaiting a trial to prove your innocence.

This may be a hypothetical case, but the circumstances are common.

Courts

In all criminal prosecutions, the accused shall enjoy the right to a speedy and public trial, by an impartial jury of the State and district wherein the crime shall have been committed, which district shall have been previously ascertained by law, and to be informed of the nature and cause of the accusation; to be confronted with the witnesses against him; to have compulsory process for obtaining witnesses in his favor, and to have the Assistance of Counsel for his defence.

That is the Sixth Amendment to the United States Constitution, part of the Bill of Rights, the absolute guarantees of life, liberty, and due process of law available to all Americans. But somehow, perhaps through the pressures of urbanization, overpopulation, and staggering crime rates, much of this one process has gone by the board. It is an exaggeration to say such processes are a rarity, but it may safely be said that they are not the normal procedure by which a person goes to prison.

Such trials do take place, attended by a great amount of publicity. Charles Manson received such a trial—it went on for eight months. The jury members were sequestered in a hotel to keep them away from publicity that might have influenced their decision. Exaggerated efforts were made to see that he received a speedy, public, and fair trial.

But this is simply not standard. At every level of operation of the American court system, you have a positive right to demand a jury trial, just as you see done in the movies or on television shows. A jury of twelve fellow citizens is selected. The state is represented by a prosecuting attorney, the defendant by a lawyer. They confront each other, brilliantly question witnesses, and plead their respective cases before the jury, which then goes off and reaches a decision. It happens this way, but in only a small percentage of cases. If every person accused of a crime demanded a jury trial, the American court system would come to a screeching halt. It is barely able to function as it is.

If you are accused of a misdemeanor, the chances of your seeing a jury are truly remote. Most likely, you will be hauled before a magistrate or some sort of police judge who may not even be a lawyer. It will be remarkable if he is not a political appointee who won his position through "connections." In corrupt places he may even have bought his judgeship.

There will be no prosecuting attorney. If you have a defense lawyer that will be all to the good, but quite unusual. Standing before the judge will be just you and the policeman who made the arrest. Everything will be informal. The judge will ask the policeman to describe how he arrested you and what you did. When the policeman is finished, the judge will ask for your side of the story. Chances are he will side with the policeman. He may be sarcastic with you and berate you in myriad ways. He may show his utter dislike for you, because of your race, hairstyle, habits, and attitudes. He has the power to acquit you, suspend your sentence, fine you, or sentence you to for up to a year in jail. The entire procedure will be over within a few minutes. You may or may not have known what went on. But whatever the decision, you are stuck with it. Tens of thousands of people are sent to jail every year by this process—to be "corrected."

But you were charged with a felony, auto theft, and this calls for a more involved procedure. Under the law, you are entitled to an "arraignment" at which the charges against you are read, and you are given an opportunity to plead innocent or guilty. If you plead innocent, a trial by jury is set for a future date; if you plead guilty, you may be sentenced on the spot, or at a later date, depending on the judge's wishes. The arraignment will bear some resemblance to a movie or television trial. A prosecuting attorney, usually a young assistant prosecutor, will be present. You will be represented by counsel, either one whom you have hired, or, if you are poor, one who has been appointed and paid by the court.

That may read like "due process of law," but I suggest that you not believe it. In large cities, which have high crime rates, dozens, scores, hundreds of people are arraigned every day. It is a cut and dried process taking no more than ten minutes. The charges are read and the plea made and that is the end of it. The judge knows absolutely nothing about the matter, and the assistant prosecutor, who has scores of cases to handle that day, knows scarcely any more. If you have a court-appointed attorney, he has a lot of similar cases, and probably could give you no more than a few minutes of his time to find out what the case was all about.

All of these very busy people have found ways to cope with their busyness so that the court system can continue to function, at least in some fashion. The most common method by far is the negotiated plea of guilty. Police have charged you with auto theft. Your attorney confers with the assistant prosecutor, who has a tremendous backlog of cases. He cannot possibly take them all to a jury trial. By the time your case comes to trial, the two witnesses against you may have left town or become less certain in their identification of you. He wants to get rid of the case.

Your attorney, knowing all this, suggests to the prosecutor that you might be willing to plead guilty to a lesser offense. They discuss the matter, and after five or ten minutes, your attorney emerges wreathed in smiles. If you will plead guilty, the prosecutor will reduce the charge to receiving stolen goods, or, if you are very lucky or the case against you very weak, to unauthorized use of property. See how much your attorney did for you!

You go to arraignment. The prosecutor reads the lesser charge. Your attorney pleads guilty on your behalf. The judge has no part in the deal. He is very busy, knows next to nothing about you or the case, but figures some sort of deal was made and he is delighted to have one less case to try. He accepts your plea and sentences you to jail or prison in accordance with the law. The prosecutor is happy—he "won" another case. The defense attorney is pleased—he got you a lesser sentence. If you did indeed steal the car, you may be delighted that your time behind bars was shortened. But what if you were innocent? What if you did not understand what was going on? What if nobody took the time to listen to you but only pressured you to take the deal? You are suddenly behind bars. If you are innocent, you wonder why you are in prison.

The negotiated plea happens hundreds of times every day

in the United States. There is a lot wrong with it aside from the issue of guilt or innocence. Under the American system of justice, a person is supposedly assumed innocent until proven guilty. The very essence of the negotiated plea is an assumption of guilt, the only issue being guilty of what? And that is negotiable. The Constitution absolutely guarantees a trial by jury before an impartial judge, but the negotiated plea affords none of that. No jury exists at all. Your innocence or guilt is determined by the assistant prosecutor, who, like the judge, knows nothing about you and very little about the crime with which you are charged. The end result is that you are removed from sight, hustled off to jail to be corrected. Others have called it "assembly-line justice."

Exceptions may be cited. Some prosecutors do not act in this way. A few are dedicated to protecting innocence and proving guilt. But in large cities, the negotiated plea is the norm.

Life magazine quoted Frank Silverstein, a young assistant district attorney in New York, on this matter. He was twenty-nine years old, a year out of law school, yet acted as judge and jury for hundreds of defendants.

The power of this job is incredible. It's more than any one man should have. Do you know what it's like to face a defendant in court and know that if he is convicted, or even if he is held in jail for trial because he can't make bail, he is going to lose his job and his family will have to go on welfare? It wouldn't be so bad if you had all day to study the facts. But there you are in court with maybe 30 cases yet to go and the judge wants to get on to the next one. You have to say something and say it fast.

Silverstein argued that it was better that a guilty defendant be convicted of *something* without a trial than be turned loose by a jury because the evidence had become too weak to get a conviction. He made no comment on whether it was better to convict the *innocent* of something.

The second method for avoiding trial is simply to delay it. You are charged with auto theft. You are arraigned and plead innocent. A date is set for your trial weeks or months later. The time comes and you arrive with your lawyer. The policeman who arrested you is there, along with the witnesses against you. Everyone waits around, greatly bored, until your case is finally called. At that point, your lawyer asks for a postponement. He hasn't had time to prepare your case; an important witness in your behalf is out of town; the lawyer has another case in court at the same time. There are many reasons for asking for a postponement. The judge agrees and reschedules the hearing for some weeks or months ahead.

Everyone is present on the next date. Again your attorney asks for a postponement. You have an illness; your mother is sick; your Aunt Harriet died; whatever. There is another postponement.

This happens two, three, four, or more times. Eventually, the witnesses become weary of going to court and waiting around for nothing. When they fail to appear it is the prosecutor who must ask for postponements. Another dodge is for *you* not to show up. A warrant will be issued for your arrest, but the chances of the undermanned court enforcement staff processing the warrant and finding you are remote.

Months, years go by in this manner until, finally, the case comes to trial. By then so much time has elapsed that the witnesses against you are no longer sure of their stories. Their testimonies can be made subject to doubt. You are acquitted.

This, too, happens every day. Consider this comment from a defense attorney:

I had a client accused of attempted murder. He shot another man several times and the victim nearly died. Over several months I managed to get the case adjourned eight or nine times. Each time the victim and the police officers were in court, but at each appearance I got a new judge and told him I needed more time to prepare. Finally, the victim just got fed up, I guess, because he stopped coming to court, and then it was the district attorney who had to ask for adjournments. After the victim failed to show up three times, the charge was finally dismissed.

There is a great deal wrong with this system of criminal justice. There is so much wrong with it that about all that can be said for it is that it does not happen this way all the time in every case. There are some people in the United States who do get fair trials. But recitation of all the good will not erase the bad that continues unabated.

The American symbol of justice is a woman, usually wearing Grecian-type robes, blindfolded, and holding scales that balance evenly. Such statues may be found atop courthouses all over the land. They are supposed to represent justice as blind, that is, the person being judged does not matter, only the crime, and that justice will therefore be dispensed equally to all. All too often American justice makes a mockery of this ideal.

American justice is not blind, it *sees*—whether or not you have money. Americans feel that the system proves itself just when a rich man goes to prison, but that rarely occurs. In the preponderance of criminal cases, if the accused comes from a family that has enough money to hire a lawyer, he will be freed on bond so he does not go to jail; he will be able to gather evidence on his side including character witnesses who will testify on his behalf; he will be able to arrange a series of postponements so that he may not be tried at all; he will be able to show the judge that his family will take care of the problem so that he may be placed on probation.

What of the poor person in this same circumstance? He will wear ragged clothes or a prison uniform. He will have been languishing in jail for weeks or months awaiting trial. He will have been unable to hire a lawyer or to develop evidence that might acquit him. He may not have a strong unified family to support him and impress the judge. No parade of character witnesses will take the stand to state what an upstanding citizen he has always been. Studies have shown that the mere fact that the defendant has been in jail rather than out on bail leads judges and juries to suspect he is guilty.

The discrepancy between the quality of justice for the rich and for the poor in the United States was shown in a study made by the President's Committee on Juvenile Delinquency and Youth Development in Contra Costa County, California, in 1966. The committee discovered that 48.2 percent of the juveniles arrested in California were released by the police after some informal handling and without charges being preferred. But in the upper-middle-class suburban community of Lafayette in Contra Costa County, 80 percent of the juveniles were released after arrest. Of the total juveniles arrested in California, 46.5 percent were referred to a juvenile court. In Lafayette, only 17.9 percent were referred to such a court. Of those who were sentenced to institutions, the California average was 5.3 percent. In Lafayette it was 1.3 percent. The comparisons would doubtlessly have been even more odious had Lafayette been compared with a black ghetto such as Watts in Los Angeles. The report concluded:

This data clearly indicate that the . . . adjustments without benefit of the formal agencies of juvenile justice for middle class suburban youth at the law enforcement level is considerably above the national and state averages.

It is not documented statistically, but it is uniformly believed that juvenile crimes, such as vandalism, are repaired privately among the affluent. The victim talks to the parent of the offender. There is family punishment. Restitution is made. This sort of thing is simply far less common in the sprawling ghettos of America's cities.

Again there are no supporting statistics, but it is widely felt, that judges tend to grant probation to an offender who comes from a respected and affluent family. When the offender comes from a lower-class family, there is a pronounced tendency to institutionalize him for his own "good," despite the overwhelming evidence that these institutions more often lead to further crime than to correction.

There is no shortage of illustrations of the difference money (and race) makes to the offender. Here are two cases I remember as a newspaperman in Baltimore. A black Maryland teen-ager from a poor section of Baltimore was part of a gang that robbed a store. In the course of the crime, a resisting storekeeper was shot and killed by one of the youths, who, without the subject's knowledge, had a gun. Even though the young man had never been in trouble before, he was tried in adult criminal court, convicted, and sentenced to life imprisonment at the Maryland House of Correction.

Some time later a twenty-four-year-old southern Maryland tobacco farmer, the son of a prominent businessman and former state official, was tried for assault, resisting arrest, and manslaughter. While drunk at a fashionable society ball, he had taunted a fifty-one-year-old hotel barmaid (the mother of eleven) with racist insults, and had struck her with a steel-topped cane because she was slow in delivering a drink. She collapsed and died. The judge sentenced him to six months in the county jail—after having allowed him to remain free until his trial so he could oversee the harvesting of his crops.

A study in Texas showed that college youths "enjoyed relative immunity" to crimes that put poor people behind bars. The investigators concluded:

Whether a man becomes a confirmed criminal may well depend less on what he does to society than on what society does to him. Pranks that cause a college student some uncomfortable moments in the Dean's office may send an East Side youth to the reformatory. Unlawful possession of a revolver may result in a warning to a suburban home owner, a prison sentence to a tenement dweller. Taking a sum of money as "honest graft" in business or public life is vastly different from taking the same amount from a cash register. . . . It is perhaps less important to show that good citizens are not always good than that these same citizens can commit crimes and still become eminent scientists, intelligent parents, leading teachers, artists and social workers, or prominent business executives.

Worse, the poor offender ends up in an institution that makes such careers all but impossible for him.

But the poor are not without their resources. Exconvict

Kenny Jackson, who now speaks to young people in schools in the New York area, often includes this story:

There's a few requirements that you need just to make it [crime] a day's outing. Have your mother come with you [to court] and have her cry. Now the better she cries, the better your chances are of getting out of Children's Court. My mother was renowned throughout the world as one of the greatest criers that ever lived. I was placed on probation. Then I got locked up again, and I was reinstated to probation. I was always being reinstated, and nothing was ever being done to change me because my mother was crying.

Perhaps no greater parody on American justice has ever been uttered than that.

There are many inequities in the American justice system. Unless they are poor and black, first offenders are not usually sent to prison. Most judges (not all!) are hesitant to impose imprisonment on young people. They try to devise some method of reform short of imprisonment. The offender—even for a second, third, or fourth time—is granted probation, ordered to repay what he has stolen or repair the damage he has done.

A large segment of the American population believes this is simple humanity, giving a person a chance to admit his mistakes and to reform. Another large segment calls this "coddling" and feels that offenders should be put behind bars at once and made to feel pain so they will decide to reform.

Both attitudes exist among American judges, often in the same courthouse. The judge has wide latitude to look at the offender and decide what should be done with him. He can "throw the book at him" and impose the maximum sentence. He can be lenient and order the minimum sentence or he can suspend the sentence and put him on probation. It is an individual decision made by the judge. As a result there are men in prison serving half their lives while other men walk the streets under probation—and all committed essentially the same crime. It is no exaggeration to say that they may all have been sentenced in the same courthouse and even by the same judge.

From all this emerges a description of the prison convict or jail inmate. The person in jail is either there awaiting trial, convicted of nothing, or has committed a misdemeanor. If he is awaiting trial, he is undoubtedly poor, and unable to post bail.

The prison convict is most likely a repeated offender, a product of jails and probation. He has been through the corrections system many times. The mere fact of imprisonment labels him "difficult" if not incorrigible.

Arrested individuals are usually not very prepossessing, scarcely likely to arouse pity or sympathy in the observer. Rough, tough, belligerent, or sleazy, evasive exteriors are common facades.

This description was given by Dr. Karl Menninger in his book, *The Crime of Punishment*. What he sought to convey was that most men behind bars do not fit the image of the criminal as portrayed in detective stories, movies, and television. He is not some intelligent person, motivated by greed, at war against society, pitting his brains against the police who would arrest him. He is the opposite. He may be a man who sees numerous people "getting away with" crime—the racketeer who sells him "numbers" tickets and drives off in a shiny black car, the businessman who overcharges him, the well-dressed executive in the business suit who pads his expense account. He tries to do the same, but he is neither smart nor lucky, and he has neither the resources nor the know-how to protect himself against his mistakes.

His crime? At best a robbery, for it showed effort and daring. More likely it was an assault in a moment of rage, a poorly planned burglary, a purse snatching, a bungled auto theft, some cheap, poorly thought out crime that a person with any intelligence would not even have considered.

This is the typical man behind bars. To be sure, there are a handful of prominent or intelligent, college-educated criminals. James Hoffa, former head of the teamsters union, spent years behind bars for jury tampering. So did Billie Sol Estes, a businessman, for swindling. Catholic priests Daniel and Philip Berrigan became convicts for raiding draft-board offices in Maryland. But these types of persons are the exceptions. The typical convict is little, defeated, a failure even at crime, not very intelligent, poor, a member of a minority group, and terribly unlucky.

Someone wishes to reform him? He faces a simple fact. Crime *does* pay. People get away with it every second of every day. With money and a little luck, the convict could, too. The problem of corrections is somehow to change that idea.

3　The Mistakes of the Past

The person behind bars is a prisoner of time. Long, idle, un-
productive minutes drag into heavy hours, days, months, until
a man or woman has invested years of his life in uselessness.
The typical prisoner is in his twenties, a time when a person is
at the peak of his strength, health, and intellect, when he is
most able to enjoy life and cope with the problems inherited
from a generation grown old, despairing, and cynical. This
above all is the tragedy of imprisonment.

The person behind bars is also a victim of time in the
sense of history. The very building, the bars that confine him
are themselves witness to the mistaken ideas of the past. Not
all, but most prisons are old and outmoded. There are people

serving time in cells that were in use when Francis Scott Key witnessed the bombardment of Fort McHenry at Baltimore during the War of 1812 and penned the *Star Spangled Banner*. A major difficulty in reforming the prison system is that these buildings are so old and unadaptable to new ideas and programs that might help offenders.

To give one example: There is evidence that group therapy may be beneficial to certain prisoners. Convicts are gathered into small groups to talk out their attitudes and problems under the guidance of a skilled psychologist or psychiatrist. Such programs have been used successfully for years in mental institutions and by private psychotherapists. But how can group therapy be practiced in a prison that contains no room larger than an eight-by-ten-foot cell or smaller than a mess-hall?

The ideas that molded prisons can be briefly reported. Centuries ago, "enlightened" opinion was that brutal punishment would reform a man who committed a crime and deter others from doing the same. In old England, from whose roots America has grown, more then three hundred offenses were punishable by death, including stealing sheep and cutting down trees. Lesser offenses called literally for an eye for an eye and a hand for a hand. Courts routinely decreed that an eye be gouged out or a hand cut off as punishment. Mere misdemeanors called for public whippings, brandings, being dragged through the streets, and being placed in stocks, wooden devices that secured the person's hands, feet, and head and put him on public display for citizens to stone. None of these practices was exclusive to old England—they were common in early America as well.

It was the height of humanitarianism when reformers advocated imprisonment as punishment. Previously, jails had been used to house debtors, political prisoners, and others awaiting trial and more severe punishment. About the middle of the eighteenth century, jails and prisons began to be used as a means of punishment. The offender was no longer viewed as inherently evil and someone to be eliminated from society, but rather as a person who had rationally and deliberately chosen crime because it gave him pleasure or profit. If he was imprisoned, he could be reformed by suffering the pain of separation from society and isolation in which to think about himself, God, his mistakes, and how he might do better.

A typical early prison was the Eastern State Penitentiary in Pennsylvania, in which cells were so arranged that the inmate lived, worked, exercised, and ate without ever seeing or talking to a fellow prisoner.

This scheme was abandoned because such prisons were too expensive to build and operate. Their replacement was the type of prison first built at Auburn, New York, where inmates were housed in single cells, but ate and worked together. The original idea, however, was incorporated into the "Silent System." Inmates were forbidden to speak under pain of solitary confinement and severe punishment.

The Silent System is no longer practiced, although elements of it still exist in many prisons. But a person does not have to be very old to have been in a prison where it was practiced. In his poignant book, *Black Voices from Prison,* Etheridge Knight, a former convict at the Indiana State Prison who now teaches in the black studies program at the University of Pittsburgh, included the reminiscences of R. L. "Whitey" Moseley. Knight explained that Moseley had been behind bars for forty-two years. "Whitey is one of the most respected of the old-timers. He is a well-kept, self-possessed man of sixty-three, with steely gray hair and a clear gaze. I don't know what crime he was convicted of. One does not ask Whitey Moseley such questions." Here are excerpts from Moseley's remembrances:

The year was 1924, and I was twenty years old. Many men already knew it [Indiana State Prison] as twenty-three acres of venomous hate, surrounded by towering gray walls. As the grisly abode of 1,800 living dead, it seethed with raw, elemental passions spawned of colorless days and endless nights spent in a graveyard of human hope.

When the massive steel gates rolled open and a man was admitted to serve his time, his head was shorn of all hair; he was dressed in a coarse gray uniform and imprisoned in a tiny, almost bare cell. A deathly silence ruled the gloomy corridors of the prison in those days—broken only at given times by the racket of slamming cell doors in a cadence that plainly echoed the resentment stored in embittered hearts. One could feel the crushing weight of prison rule, the total suppression, as the iron jaws of the massive cellblocks worked at their ceaseless grinding on human souls. One strained his ears to catch a human sound, but there was none. All was still as the final grave. The spirit of the stoutest man felt annihilated.

The Silent System in effect then reduced everybody to using signs whenever communication was necessary. It was a piece of wry humor to raise the hand, receive a nod from the glum guard on his little raised dais in the shops, approach him and motion that one had to "go." A wooden paddle hung on a nail at his desk. The "goer" took the paddle and walked with it in hand to a two-closet affair shielded only by a halfway partition and hung the wooden paddle on the outside of the halfway door. The time that the paddle was returned to the desk indicated how long the "goer" had been absent from his task of work. There was no chance for stalling or goldbricking, for the paddle "snitched" by its very whereabouts. . . .

Tension was always at a high peak, as each man literally slaved over his task. Despite the Silent System, men did manage to communicate, for on Saturdays, in season, tier by tier of men marched to the drill ground to watch a baseball game. Under the broiling sun they sat bunched together on wooden benches, unable to smoke because smoking was forbidden anyplace save three times a night in the cell. A kind of cellblock trusty passed a light from cell to cell, carrying a flaming torch like the eternal flame used at the Olympics.

Mail and a weekly newspaper were excessively censored, with items cut out or obliterated by the censors. It was a violation of rules to have a pencil, ink, paper or anything in the tiny cells, excepting a towel, two library books, comb and a piece of soap. The walls were barren of pictures—a rocking chair, a toilet bowl, and a wash basin were the only fixtures. Attendance at ball games, two-reel movies, and chapel were compulsory.

Everybody worked. The aged mended prisoners' sox, the lame led the blind around the grounds, picking up bits of stray paper and leaves. There was, it seemed, a heartless efficiency about routines, day after endless day, year upon colorless year. There being so little for diversion, the average inmate deteriorated, suffering from mental inertia, frustrated and oppressed by the futility of his daily existence.

The book in which this was written is not old. It was published in 1970. Moseley is of an age where he could be your grandfather. He says the Silent System was not abandoned at his prison until 1933. What is important to this description is that tens of thousands of prisoners are housed in jails and prisons erected in conformance with the Silent System. Prisoners are housed in individual, isolated cells. Other facilities are designed for working, eating, or exercising. There is virtually nothing else. Even the most progressive warden, desiring to help inmates adjust to their problems so they can return to society rehabilitated, is stymied in his efforts by the very building that houses the prisoners.

Two other "reform" ideas of yesterday helped to create the prison problems of today. A century and more ago, it was decided that city life was a bad influence, leading men and women and particularly youths into crime. They would be reformed by the sunlight, fresh air, and wholesomeness of country life. Hard, regular manual labor on a farm would teach them new attitudes. The quiet, undistracted life of the countryside would return them to nature and enable them to ponder their mistakes.

Therefore, dozens, scores, hundreds of institutions were built "out in the sticks." They had high walls and guard towers—security was necessary—but they were invariably surrounded by a farm extending for thousands of acres. Inmates tended cattle, planted and harvested crops. They had plenty of sunlight and fresh air.

Today the legacy of this thinking is a millstone around the warden's neck. The warden knows that America has a large urban population. Seventy percent of Americans live in cities, which are where most offenders come from. Modern penological thought is that inmates need help and training to return to the community, so they will be better able to cope with the problems that led to their crimes in the first place. But how can the warden work out programs to involve the inmate in community activities when the prison is located fifty miles from nowhere?

One of the more promising recent innovations is the work-release program. The convict spends the night in prison, but during the day he holds a job, earning regular wages with which he supports himself and his family. These programs have been highly successful in rehabilitating offenders. But how can a warden develop more than a minimal work-release program when the nearest populated place is a bovine country village and the nearest city offering plentiful jobs is miles away?

The second ideological milestone is the notion that prisons should be profitable. The thought of a century ago—which persists today—was that prisoners should work. The discipline of work would be beneficial to them and they could learn a trade that they would use upon returning to civilian life. Moreover, the products grown or made by the prisoners could be sold for a profit, at the very least enough to defray the high cost of operating the prison.

This idea, which became highly popular by the 1930's, ran into instant difficulty. Labor unions and businessmen objected to the competition of prison industries. Why should an honest, law-abiding worker be out of a job because a convict was making products in competition with him? There was an outcry, which state and federal politicians heard.

A solution was at hand. Prison inmates would work and even earn a profit by doing work that did not compete with private industry. The principal buyer of the products of prison industries would be the government itself. No one could object if government saved the taxpayers money by having unpaid prison labor make products or perform services that the government needed.

Thus was born the infamous manufacture of automobile license plates. Virtually all license tags are made in prisons.

The convicts are kept busy, the state governments save money, and there is no competition with private industry. Beautiful. The only problem is that a man may spend twenty years in prison and become the world's most proficient maker of license plates, but where is he going to get a job making license plates after he is released?

Furniture refinishing is another large prison industry. Inmates repair the desks and chairs used in government offices. This has a certain usefulness to a man, but furniture refinishing is hardly a large industry offering employment to very many people, no matter how good they are at it. Inmates also print government documents. Printing is a useful trade to a released inmate. Other common prison industries are farming, making road signs, manufacturing gloves, shoes, and mattresses used in prisons and other institutions, making brushes, and reconditioning tires. Some progressive prisons have established industries and training programs in such fields as plastics, radio repair, electronics, auto repair, and mechanics. But the equipment used is so outmoded that the inmate's "training" is close to useless when he is released.

The idea that prisons should be profitable is largely outmoded—the Cummins Prison Farm in Arkansas being a notable exception. But productive work for the inmate is still the goal, even when it is called training. The directors of prison industries like to report how much money they make in the course of a year. But nobody considers such programs very beneficial to the prisoners in terms of rehabilitation. They may learn the discipline of work, but does not learning take five, ten, and twenty years? The skills they learn have only limited usefulness at best, and they are paid as little as ten and twenty cents an hour. They are hardly learning the value of hard, useful work for which they are paid as other men are.

Reformers developed many ideas intended to rehabilitate prisoners and help them become useful citizens. The oldest of these is encouraging religion. Even under the Silent System prisoners went to compulsory church services. Reformers believed that practicing religion, be it Catholicism, Judaism, or Protestantism, would develop a sense of right and wrong, an awareness of morality among convicts. This could not but help them reform.

To this day, religion is a powerful force in most prisons. Clergymen hold services regularly and work with prisoners individually and in groups. Many convicts are converted to religion and are baptized. And it is not necessarily Christianity or Judaism. The Black Muslim religion, founded by Elijah Mohammed and embracing a form of the Muslim religion, has long been successful among convicts and has won many of its adherents in prisons. The most famous was the late Malcolm X, who as a convict became a Black Muslim and was later an inspirational leader among his people.

Classification has become another major reform idea. A long-standing cause of abuse in prisons was the lumping together of all prisoners: young first offenders with experienced criminals, the repentant with the incorrigible, the insane, the mentally retarded, the perverted. Efforts were begun to separate these people through classification. Training schools were built for the very young, reformatories for young men who could still be saved, penitentiaries for older, "hardened," and "incorrigible" criminals. Even within individual institutions efforts were made to separate inmates by age, education, health, type of offense, and mental attitudes. These efforts have never been wholly successful, but classification has long been considered a major prison reform.

A variety of programs were established to help the prisoner adjust to life behind bars and to contribute to his reformation. Recreation is the oldest of these. Whereas even under the Silent System, inmates attended ball games, prisons today offer a wide range of recreational activities. There are organized athletic leagues that provide for inmate teams from several prisons to play opposite one another as well as against nonconvicts. Cards, chess, and billiards are available, and libraries and other facilities are at hand to help inmates cope with the boredom of prison life.

Educational facilities have been developed, especially in large, progressive prisons, which employ staff teachers. Educational programs include everything from beginning reading and writing classes for illiterates to high school and even college courses. Inmates can attend classes or study independently, but the emphasis is on vocational courses.

Effort is made to care for the health of the prisoner. Almost every prison has an infirmary with doctors and nurses on duty, and in large institutions there are good-sized hospitals. Most prisons offer psychiatric services, with psychologists and psychiatrists employed to treat patients who have mental or emotional problems. Those who are seriously disturbed are transferred to mental hospitals for treatment. Social services are also offered, providing sociologists and social workers who try to help inmates solve marriage and family problems. One of the most important social-service functions is to assist the inmate who is about to be released to find a job and a place to live. Counselors are employed to talk to inmates and help them with their problems.

These services are considered crucial to modern penology. In practice, however, they do not come close to achieving their desired goals. At best they are a thin veneer overlaid upon the Silent System. Most prisons do not have enough money to hire an adequate staff of doctors, teachers, psychologists, sociologists, and other experts. The salaries offered are so low that it is difficult to attract qualified people or to keep the good ones very long, and there is a high turnover rate among such employees. Once the expertly trained staff member gains experience, he often quits, either for a higher paying job or because he is discouraged.

Even if there were enough teachers, psychologists, counselors, and other such professional personnel, two factors would still undermine their effectiveness. Old ideas from the past linger. First, prison administrators are obsessed with *custody*. The most important function of prisons is still to keep the offender behind the stone walls. The largest group of employees is comprised of guards, armed with rifles and shotguns, and the prisoner is seldom out of the sight of such weapons. An escape by prisoners must be avoided at all costs. Despite the publicity an escape receives, there are relatively few. Prisons are very effective in maintaining custody.

Another goal from the past is *order*. Prison riots also make headlines in the newspapers, but again there are relatively few. Inmates live a highly restricted and regimented life. They are locked in cells most of the time, then herded like sheep to work, eat, play, or attend school. Extensive rules restrict their movements, speech, and actions. They can do little without written or oral permission. They are denied freedom, not only by the walls of the prison, but by the rules of the institution itself.

Foremost punishment for breaking rules or being a troublemaker is loss of "good time." If a prisoner abides by the rules and causes no trouble, his sentence can be reduced by as much as a third. Sentenced to ten years, he can be released in six or seven—even without parole—because he has been a "good" prisoner and not caused trouble. The incentive for the inmate is obvious. He will get out a lot quicker if he simply obeys the rules, makes no trouble, submerges his independence and individuality and frustration, and accepts the highly regimented life.

But there is also an obvious difficulty with this "good time" system of regimentation. American life, outside of prisons and possibly the armed forces, is not regimented. Living in America calls for freedom of choice, making decisions, resisting temptations, and self-discipline. An adult acts on his own with only minimal help from family and friends. No one tells him when to go to bed or get up, what to eat, how to behave with other people. Making these and countless other choices himself is the essence of freedom. A person ends up behind bars either because he made the wrong choices or because he did not know or was ill-equipped to make the right ones. But what in the regimentation of prison life trains a person to recognize and make the right choices? If everything is done for him on a rigid schedule, how can he learn to do for himself? If he is moved about as part of a herd of cattle, how can he learn to be an individual?

Nearly all efforts at rehabilitation of prisoners is further undermined by the attitudes of the inmates and the entire culture that exists in prison.

4 Life Behind Bars

No one knows what really goes on in prison. The most able, experienced, and dedicated warden can only say how many prisoners he has, where they are at a given moment, and what tasks they are doing or supposed to be doing. He can describe rehabilitative programs and cite an impressive array of statistics. But he will admit he has only the most general idea of the prisoners' attitudes and the inside society they have developed.

Prisoners have their own culture. They have their own rules of conduct, which are entirely separate from the prison rules and often their exact opposite. They have their leaders and followers. They have ways of judging inmates and of punishing them, as well as ways to gratify their pleasures and vices.

To a great extent, this type of structure inevitably develops among groups of people. But much of it is fostered by the "good time" system used in prisons to maintain order. Inmates may hate each other, they may disagree on most everything, but they will unite in a common goal—the need for good time. Nothing must occur to threaten the good time of a single inmate. All that happens must be hidden from guards and prison officials, who must have only an impression of orderly compliance with the prison rules. Whatever else happens must remain unknown to them.

The expression that describes this attitude is "do your own time." Each prisoner views himself as an island unto himself. He is alone in a building housing hundreds or thousands of men and he will remain aloof from all others. If he has problems with another inmate, he will find ways to solve them himself. If he is weak, he will suffer the consequences. If he is strong, he will survive. But under no circumstances will he appeal to the prison officials for help. Such an action would endanger his good time, for inmate retaliation would be swift and sure. His chances for parole might be lessened because he is "getting into trouble." Besides, no prison officer can really help him. He is alone.

Every prison has a "pecking order," an expression that stems from studies among chickens. It was discovered that chickens in a barnyard quickly arrange themselves into a hierarchy. At the top is a chicken that can peck all others. At the bottom is a poor wretched creature that is pecked by all the others.

The prison pecking order is based on several factors. One

is the crime the man committed. Held in greatest respect are those tough, clever criminals who got away with many crimes and were not easily caught. A bank robber might rank high on the list, or an expert safe cracker, jewel thief, forger, or embezzler. Sex criminals rank low. Inmates have no more respect for a child rapist than does anyone else.

An inmate may win respect for his "brains," not necessarily in the sense of intelligence, but in cleverness. Outside connections may win him influence. He is a member of a criminal organization or an associate of a famous criminal. If he has power on the outside, he gains power inside. Respect can be gained by an older man who has spent a lot of time in prison and is "savvy" about prison life and how to get by with minimum discomfort. The few individuals who have intelligence and education can be respected, if they abide by the rules of the inmate society.

Toughness also can place a man high in the hierarchy. He will do whatever is necessary at whatever cost to defend himself; he has friends who will aid him; he is so knowledgeable about the prison and its staff that he cannot be "messed with."

The 1967 report of the President's Commission on Law Enforcement and the Administration of Justice described the men at the top of the hierarchy as "politicians" or "big shots." This "elite inmate group," the commission said,

are those who have not only earned respect among their fellows but also have developed rapport with staff. These tend to be persons with extensive institutional experience who have been tested in interactions with other inmates sufficiently that they are neither readily "pushed around" by their fellows nor distrusted as "stool pigeons."

The Commission continued:

They have also been tested sufficiently by staff to be assigned jobs in offices or other locations where they can communicate readily with staff and often have access to institutional records. Because of their possession of "inside" information and their access to staff, they can command considerable deference from other inmates. However, they can also convince inmates that they generally work for their interest through manipulating the staff. They are thus the leadership in the inmate caste and the middleman between the staff and inmates.

Other descriptions of the convict caste system indicate that the men at the top also conduct the prison rackets. They are sometimes called "racketeers." Because of their work with the staff and their outside connections, they are the source of drugs and other contraband smuggled into the prison. They are the "loan sharks," that is, they loan money to inmates. They send messages between inmates or to the outside and perform other surreptitious services—all for a fee.

Beneath the politicians, the Commission reported, are the "right guys" or "straights."

Among them a few may ultimately move to politician status. Most of them, however, are not routinely thrown into very personal contact with staff. Should they have an opportunity for private communication with staff, they are likely to be suspected by inmates.

At the lowest echelon are "sex offenders, the physically weak and immature, the mentally disordered and retarded," as the Commission described them. Here, too, are many of the aggressive inmates, men with such a tendency to violence they are feared by inmates and staff alike.

There is very little in this convict society to "correct" an offender by preparing him to assume a normal role in society upon his release. It might be argued that the "big shots" are learning leadership, but they lead by manipulating both the prison staff and inmates. There is doubtlessly a certain value in being able to manipulate people in a person's work or community activities, but most people on the outside resist being manipulated. Leadership is derived from knowledge, skill, money, hard work, and the ability to inspire others. Clever manipulation is of short-term value without these other assets.

Describing the prison hierarchy is useful, but it still does not tell very much about what goes on in prisons. Again, no one knows or is telling all. But there is some information.

Perhaps the most revealing descriptions of prison life were made during the summer of 1969 at a remarkable conference held on the campus of St. John's College in Annapolis, Maryland. About one hundred lawyers, judges, prosecutors, policemen, prison officials, state legislators, and interested citizens joined twenty-one prison inmates in no-holds-barred sessions. Everyone was free to speak his mind without penalty. A "pious platitude" or an obviously untrue statement would be hooted down by participants. A feature of the sessions were playlets, called "psychodramas," in which inmates, police, judges, and prison officials acted out their real-life roles or sometimes changed places. The raw sores of prison life were revealed. In attendance was reporter Richard Hammer who presented a verbatim account of a psychodrama in the *New York Times Magazine*.

The psychodrama consisted of a situation created in ad-

vance, but the dialogue, the words spoken, were created by
the participants at the time of presentation. The situation was
the arrival in prison of a new con, a first offender sentenced to
four years for assault. A young, blond correctional officer was
selected to play this role. Hammer said he looked indeed as if
he could be in that position. The inmates who processed him
into prison were played by real cons. The only other roles
were two prison officials, a guard and a counselor. All were
played by men whose real-life roles these were. Here is Hammer's description of the play.

   The drama began as "Scag," a black inmate who supposedly
worked as a runner in the prison storeroom, led the new con,
"Frank," from the storeroom, where he'd been issued prison
clothes and other gear, to the tier where he could be locked into a
cell.

Scag: You know anybody here, anybody can help you?

Frank: (shaking his head) No, I don't know anybody.

Scag: Not nobody at all?

Frank: Nobody. I don't think I belong here.

Scag (laughs): That's what everybody says. You know, you gonna
   need some protection.

Frank: Protection? From what?

Scag: Man, you is gonna be approached.

Frank: What for?

Scag: Man, I ain't got to tell you.

Frank: Well, I don't want any part of it.

Scag: You ain't got no choice.

Frank: If they come to me, I'll fight.

Scag (laughs): You can't fight three, four men at a time.

Frank: What can I do?

Scag: Man, you can avoid it.

Frank: How?

Scag: You can pick somebody to protect you. . . . You got any money?

Frank: No. But I've got a ring and a watch.

Reaching the tier that contains Frank's cell, Scag holds a mumbled conference with Slim, a black inmate assigned as a runner in the tier.

Scag: We got a new chicken here.

Slim: Yeah, what we gonna do with him?

Scag: I'll tell you. I'm gonna play his friend. You make him think he's got to turn to me to protect him from you.

Slim: Yeah, that's right. I'll scare him right to you and we'll split what he's got. Only don't do like you did the last time and hit me when you're protecting him.

Scag: Don't worry, we'll play this cool.

As Scag leaves, Slim explains prison life to Frank, telling him that he can order once a week from the commissary and that he must come out of his cell immediately when the bell rings for a meal or an exercise period in the yard or he will be locked in again. Slim offers to give Frank a pack of cigarettes in exchange for two packs after Frank has received his order from the commissary. Then a bell rings and Slim patrols the tier, chanting, "Yard time. Yard Time."

The scene shifts to the crowded prison yard, and when Frank appears there are whistles. "Say, man," says one con, "that's a real sweetie." Another yells: "Hey, baby, I think you need a protector." The action then moves back to the cell tier.

Slim: Where you been?

Frank: In the yard.

Slim: How come you didn't tell me you was going?

Frank: I did.

Slim: Man, I says you didn't! You callin' me a liar?

Frank: No, I thought . . .

Slim: Man, you want to go someplace, you tell me. Whenever you
    go someplace, you don't go without you let me know, dig?
Frank: Why are you jumping all over me?
Slim: Man, you is askin' for it. I gonna come in that cell with you
    and lock the door you don't watch out.

Scag suddenly appears, telling Slim to leave the new inmate
alone. After Slim wanders off, Scag offers to take Frank into the
yard during the next exercise period and walk around with him,
explaining: "That'll let everybody know I'm protecting you."
He says it will cost a carton of cigarettes a week. Frank says he
will think about it and stays in his cell during the next few exercise periods. A few days later, against Slim's urgent advice, he
insists upon seeing an officer.

Frank: It seems there are all these guys who want to be my bud-
    dies. They want to protect me. But they want cigarettes and they
    seem to want my watch and ring and shoes, too. And they seem
    to be able to do anything they want and nobody stops them.
Guard: When did all this start? When did they approach you?
Frank: As soon as I got in here.
Guard: Can you identify them?
Frank: I'm afraid. I don't want it to get back to them.
Guard: Well, anytime you want to tell me anything, you just ask,
    I'll come. You just ask. We'll protect you.
Frank: I'm scared to tell.

The realization that the guards cannot effectively protect him
sends Frank back to Scag. At the next yard call, they go out together and Scag introduces Frank to other cons, among whom
blacks outnumber whites by more than two to one.

The play action was interrupted at this point. Several of
the convicts at the conference were asked what they were feeling. Hammer reported these answers:

I'm feeling that colored guys have all the goodies. I feel like they must feel out in the streets. I'm a minority in here, and I'd like a crack at that goody.

I don't care what Scag or the rest of the black guys do as long as they don't touch my man.

I've got a feeling of fear. I know what happens to young cons like him; it happened to me.

He's a white boy, and I don't care what happens to him.

The action of the psychodrama resumes in the office of a counselor with whom Frank has requested an interview.

Frank: I've had some weird things happen since I came in here. There's a lot of homosexuals running around loose and they all seem to be looking at me.

Counselor: Well, what would you like us to do?

Frank: I don't know. I think I'm more afraid of the inmates here than I am of the institution itself, and I thought it would be the other way.

Counselor: What do they want?

Frank: Everything I've got. My watch, my ring, my shoes, all my personal possessions. Can I send them home?

Counselor: Yes. If you give them to me I can have them sent home for you.

Frank: They want my tail, too.

Counselor: I'm afraid I can't send that home. You want to tell me who these guys are who are doing these things to you?

Frank: If I tell you, what will happen to me?

Counselor: We'll try to protect you.

Frank: How?

Counselor (burst out): I'll adopt you! . . . Seriously, the only assurance I can give you is close supervision.

The psychodrama ended there, amid shouts from the convicts in the audience. "Man, you can't give him no protection. He'll have boiling coffee thrown at him even if you lock him up in solitary," said one. "He ain't got no assurance. You think his only salvation is in protection and custody, but that won't work. Somebody'll get to him."

"Maybe you'd put him in B-3, where they keep all the sissies," said another con, "and then he'd be branded one, and he'd be branded a rat, too, and that wouldn't be no protection."

"There's a million ways to get to him," a third convict warned. "We'd be in contact with him and that would be that."

Another said: "Nothing anybody can do will make any difference because it's a jungle we live in. The only ones who can do anything for him or against him are the other inmates."

Hammer said one of the prison administrators asked the actor who played Slim if he would have protected Frank for a guaranteed parole?

Slim stared at him, "For a guaranteed parole, Man, I guess so."

Another con leaped up: "And who would protect Slim? Then who would protect the next guy and the next? You gonna let us all out on parole to protect this one guy?"

This psychodrama reveals a great deal about prison life, although hardly all. There *is* violence among inmates. Men are beaten, maimed, and sometimes killed. But except in a few truly backward prisons, there is a lot less violence than the public thinks. What does exist is the *threat* of violence, the unspoken knowledge of an inmate that violence can come to him if he breaks the silent system of the prisoners and "rats."

Some variety of rackets operate in most, perhaps every prison. There is apparently a sizable amount of homosexuality practiced. Some is by consenting adults. But there are men who prey upon the weak and immature, coercing them with violence, threats, and bribery.

Racism flourishes. Inmates separate themselves by race, although the prison staff does not. Predictable racial attitudes abound, complete with insults, tensions, and some violence.

Most importantly, the psychodrama shows the utter powerlessness of prison officials to do anything at all about such situations. This prison subculture is unlikely to "correct" anyone. As the Commission on Law Enforcement stated, "The existence of an illegitimate subculture of inmate relationships, often founded on violence and corruption, intensifies the criminal's commitment to these values."

The prison subculture, its "silent system," the concept of "good time" and "doing your own time" are still not the major reason prisons are so futile and self-defeating. The major problems of prison life are the regimentation, suffocating boredom, and shattering indifference. There are several excellent accounts of these. I have chosen the account of Etheridge Knight in *Black Voices from Prison* because he has the soul of a poet (he credits poetry with bringing him "back to live" after he "died" in prison) and is an excellent writer.

Today the walls of the Indiana State Prison are forty-three feet high; they are gray stone and concrete, surrounding 23 acres of land. Inside these walls are 2,000 men, black, white and brown, ranging in age from sixteen to eighty-three. The average age is 36. The prison boasts one ex-policeman, one ex-Justice of the Peace, a bank embezzler, and four college graduates. The vast majority, however, come from the lower economic level and are small-time burglars, stickup artists and forgers. Lifers make up the largest group; there are 450.

And what do these men do inside these walls? It's simple, maddeningly simple: At six o'clock in the morning a whistle blows. They get up and wash their faces. At six-fifteen, a bell rings, and they march off to the prison mess hall and eat a breakfast of, say, oatmeal, prunes, bread and coffee. They leave the mess hall in a line and drop their spoons in a bucket by the door, watched over by a "screw." They march to their shops—say the Tag Shop, climb upon a stool and dip license plates into a tank of paint until nine-thirty. A bell rings; they smoke. A bell rings; they go back to work.

At eleven-thirty a bell rings again. They stop work, wash up, march back to their shelters. At twelve o'clock a bell rings in the cellhouse; they walk to the mess hall where they eat, say, a meal of white beans, frankfurters and cornbread. They leave the mess hall, drop their spoons into a bucket and, in line, go back to work. The morning performance is repeated. At four-thirty a whistle blows; they march to supper and then into their cellhouse for the night. Maddeningly simple.

Most of the ancient buildings in which the men work and live are made of red bricks, with green tile roofs. They rise stark and bare, ornamented only with steel-barred windows, deep-set and elongated windows that make the sides of the building look like sad-faced clowns. There are four cellhouses: A, B, C, and D; and two dormitories, I and G. Each cellhouse shelters approximately 400 men, and the two dormitories about 400.

One of the oldest and most famous cellhouses is "B." It was built in 1907 and was once the home of John Dillinger. The first thing that strikes you about the cellhouse is its immensity. An oblong barnlike building, it stretches more than two-thirds of a city block, and the glaring light bulbs strung along the walkways in front of the cells give the illusion of even greater distance. The cells are stacked five tiers high, ranging back to back down the center of the cellhouse with their fronts gaping at the outer walls.

Coming in from work, the men file up the iron stairs like long lines of worker ants, their heavy steps unlike the sounds made by any other group of moving men. As they reach their respective tiers, they break off, and each man goes to his cell. A bell rings twice, and at the front end of each a guard begins to lock the cells and count the men. Then it is quiet time, nervous time, until after mail call, which will occur in about thirty minutes.

Knight then described the cells:

The cells are ten feet long and six feet wide. (Although the practice has been discontinued, two men were once assigned to some of these cells.) On the door of each cell is a card, bearing the inmate's name, number and job assignment. Each cell contains a toilet bowl, a wash basin, a cot, a set of earphones [to listen to the radio], and whatever small furniture the inmates can either make or scrounge. For the past few years, the men have been permitted to paint their own cells, choosing their own colors. Some men keep their cells extraordinarily neat. Precise. Others barely manage to pass the occasional inspection by the cellhouse officer. By and large a man is allowed to arrange his cell as he sees fit.

And what do the men do in their cells? One young man, a muscle boy, is doing push-ups. Two hundred a night. Another man is answering a letter he has just received. One man is pacing his cell, stopping every now and then to crack his knuckles. Another is lying on his bunk listening to his earphones. Another is standing, gripping the bars and calling down the gallery to his buddy. Another is already in bed, his knees drawn up toward his chest, his blanket pulled over his head. Most of the men read books: westerns, blood and sex detective mysteries, Gothic romances, and current booklist novels, in that order.

Some men have lived in the same cells for eight, ten and twelve years. The pressures are heavy, and the sounds made at night by 400 caged men are lonely and empty. A clacking typewriter, a flushing toilet, a futile curse, and drifting, distorted music from a radio. An inmate spends from fourteen to sixteen hours a day in his cell. Soon it becomes, in truth, his home.

This existence—and what more can it be called?—accords with the old notion that a man could be reformed by loneliness. If he sat in his cell and thought about himself and his crimes, he would repent and go straight. No one has ever proved that idea has any validity at all. But granting that it might does the process take as long as years upon tortuous years, a whole lifetime?

What does the prisoner feel?

For an answer let us turn again to that remarkable conference at St. John's College. Its high point came when a group of judges, lawyers, policemen, and other officials changed places with inmates in prison. Every effort was made to keep prison officials from knowing those men who arrived at the prison gate handcuffed and shackled in a police van were not ordinary prisoners. They were checked in, stripped, and made to sit naked on wooden benches, while being interviewed. An examination by flashlight was made under their arms, between their legs and of other hairy parts of the body. An inmate clerk explained: "We're looking for crabs, narcotics, you know, things like that."

The "convicts" were showered, given prison uniforms, photographed in different positions, or "mugged," fingerprinted, and asked detailed questions about their lives. Then, they were led to cells and locked in.

Richard Hammer described some of the reactions. An elderly, white-haired state representative sank onto his cot, put his elbows on his knees and buried his head in his hands. He said later:

I can't tell you what this did to me spiritually. I knew that any time I wanted to get out, all I had to do was yell and they would come and let me loose. What if I had known that I couldn't get out, that I was to be locked in there for years.

A judge who had sentenced scores of men to prison was certain that he had been identified by inmates. "I didn't know whether I was going to get a knife or just be pointed out to everyone else." He asked for release after a couple of hours.

Another judge was "framed" by a guard who had been let in on the deception. He planted a knife in the judge's cell. The jurist was pulled from the lunch line and thrown into solitary confinement in the "hole" next to a black convict who was lying on his cell floor, his legs in the air, screaming. Reporter Hammer said the judge later reported he had not heard a thing.

After a half hour in the hole, the judge came before a five-man disciplinary panel. Here is Hammer's description of the incident:

The judge was dressed in prison slacks and shirt, white sox without shoes; his hair was tousled, his face distraught.

The board chairman asked, "Do you know why you're here?"

"They told me you found a knife in my cell."

"That's right. Can you tell us how it got there?"

"No, I can't think how."

"Did you bring it with you?"

"No. Somebody must have put it there."

"When did you get here?"

"This morning."

"Do you know anybody in here?"

"No."

"Does anybody in here have anything against you?"

"No."

"Then why would somebody plant a knife in your cell?"

The judge, knowing he was innocent, was sentenced to 30 days in the hole.

A civilian-inmate described the prison as a "decayed military school"—no morale, no screens on the windows, razor blades in his cell, splinters of steel in his food, a total lack of communication between the staff and the prisoners and everywhere he looked "there were flaming faggots [homosexuals] making assignations."

No account was more poignant than that of a high-ranking police officer who became a pretend inmate. He met a convict who seemed familiar, then discovered he had first met the boy as an eleven-year-old school truant. Later the boy had stabbed his mother during an argument and become involved in one kind of trouble after another, finally going to prison for murder. Said the officer:

I wondered if maybe I couldn't have done something, back then, to have prevented all this. But I'll tell you one thing: I'm going to be a better cop because of this. And I'll tell you something else: nobody's going to work for me for 18 years without going into an institution this way again. Every man under me is going to spend a day in prison.

Hammer felt that a judge deserved the last word:

This is a jungle. And if all the guys inside come out as they have to live in there, pretty soon we're all going to be living in that jungle. We'd better do something and we'd better do it damn fast.

This remarkable experiment indicates how innocent, respected men in the community feel during a single day in prison. But what of the offender? What goes on in his mind? The writings of inmates indicate there is a variety of emotions, rage, bitterness, a violent need for vengeance, rebellion, despair, repentance. Some become violent, trouble-making prisoners and suffer the consequences of prison discipline. Others give up and become weak and pliable, little more than human vegetables. But the best and perhaps the most reach some sort of accommodation with prison. They bend to the rules and find a way to survive not just physically, but spiritually as well. Many take pride in the fact that they have endured. At least they were not broken.

The typical inmate goes through various reasonably similar psychological phases in prison. These were described some years ago in *The Atlantian,* a magazine published by inmates at the Federal Penitentiary in Atlanta.

The prisoner's first reaction is that prison is a "dreadful place," with high walls, steel bars, and watchful guards. His reaction is one of loneliness. Then comes ROUTINE. "Life goes on, even in a penitentiary, and we become accustomed to the clanging bells, bugle calls, regimentation, lack of privacy, loss of initiative, deprivation of individuality, menial work." But soon comes a period of ADJUSTMENT.

The inmate begins to participate in the prison programs. Forty percent become active in some phase of the recreation program, 23 percent in education, 20 percent in religion, 12 percent in the trade training program.

We seek something to keep us occupied—and some of us even admit to ourselves that we would like to better ourselves . . . and we all become aware that we are coming closer to completing one-third of our sentence and with it, the chance for Parole. At night, alone with our thoughts in the darkened cell, some of us vow that if we are granted Parole, we'll make good.

The parole is denied. Eighty-five per cent of us are turned down by the U.S. Board of Parole—and no one seems surprised by their decisions. . . . Our institutional record has been good, our program participation had been excellent and sincere . . . and the numbing feeling after denial soon dims and is succeeded by action.

The inmate elects to go to work in the prison industries. He works hard, and is paid little, but is able to save some money. More important, he earns additional "good time."

But working in the industries, the inmate no longer has the time to participate in the recreational, educational, and other programs.

We simply work, read, listen to our earphones and sleep. . . . After awhile, we become restless with the monotonous existence and we acquire a hobby interest. . . . We write, we draw, we carve and sometimes in desperation, we buy yarn with which we crochet!

This sort of activity continues until two-thirds of the sentence is passed and the inmate can begin to plan for his release, which he has won because he has earned "good time."

Remember the above was written at a federal prison, the best in the nation.

Virtually all prisoners, contrary to public belief, do not claim to be innocent. They know they are guilty of *some* crime. It may be human nature or the effects of imprisonment, but most prisoners come to regret their crimes. They are sincerely sorry for their past actions and mistakes and resolve to do better. Since this is an acknowledged aim of prisons, it must be said they are very successful in reforming men's attitudes.

But does the prison system take advantage of this reformation in attitude?

Etheridge Knight, again in *Black Voices from Prison,* includes the "testimony" of Willian Healy, another inmate at the Indiana State Prison. Healy wrote:

Once the full implication and weight of my sentence crashed into my consciousness . . . the prayers, rank with human bargaining and irreverence, began to fall from my lips: "Oh, if only you would cut me loose. . . ." And I also turned to that beautiful prayer first recited by St. Bernard in honor of the Blessed Virgin, the *Memorare.* It opens: "Remember, O most gracious Virgin Mary, that never was it known that anyone who fled to thy protection, implored thy help and sought thine intercession, was left unaided . . ."

This insipid fervor was used to stoke the fires of hope, and it lasted three nights as I religiously recited the prayer again and again; but repetition also to give up praying again, to find in rejection a new justification. . . . I felt more like a Christian inside the lion than in the lion's den; for when the inner flame flickered in anguish and loneliness, prayer was extinguished.

There is more to prayer than supplication; I can recall the advice given to me by a priest ("I don't seem to pray well, father") who urged me to pray in thanksgiving for blessings which I'd received, in adoration and, often, penitently to beg forgiveness. In this respect I know that I didn't pray then; I know that I haven't prayed like this for a very long time.

So this is prison! Its storied existence is a legend commercialized by book and film, a fictitious narrative depicting prison as a place full of men hard and calloused beyond belief, who have committed acts against a society which, in turn, has sentenced them to this place where a man's life is given up to serving time.

Yet, prison's self-image is perpetuated not by the men lodged in penal institutions (although many men have died here because of it, believing in the legend), but through an atmosphere which demands the continuation of both guilt and punishment. *The great tragedy of our penal system, also its interior weakness, is its promise to be always indifferent, never conferring upon an individual the conditional absolution.* . . . (Emphasis added.)

Is Healy unusual? He certainly is in his ability to express himself. Most people, in or out of prison, do not write so well. But is he expressing an attitude common to many prisoners? Is he correct in saying that most prisoners want simple forgiveness and a chance to do better? If he is, then he has pinpointed a serious deficiency in our prison system, for it is extremely difficult for the offender to gain that forgiveness by getting out of prison and being accepted into society.

5 After Prison

There are only four ways for a man to get out of prison alive.
One is by some process of law. He is found to be wrongly
convicted or he is granted a new trial or a governor com-
mutes his sentence. All of these occur, and rather frequently,
but they are beyond the province of this book.

Another way is to escape, by breaking out of the walls or
by walking away after earning status as a "trusty." Escapes
are made, although not very often. Most escapees are recap-
tured within minutes, hours, or days. For a man to be at large
for weeks is unusual.

Occasionally a man escapes for years and reforms, living
a life free from crime. Such an incident came to light when I

was a young reporter covering the Ohio State Reformatory at Mansfield. A solid, responsible citizen living in New Jersey was unmasked as a man who had escaped from the reformatory more than twenty years before. During those years he had married, raised a family, and held a good job. I do not recall the circumstances that led to his being discovered, and it does not matter. Caught he was.

The state of Ohio immediately began legal proceedings to return the man to the reformatory. I remember vividly a discussion I had with Arthur Glattke, the superintendent of the reformatory.

"It seems to me," I said, "that the entire purpose of prison is to reform a man so that he can live a useful life. This man in New Jersey clearly showed he could do this. Imprisonment was a huge success. What sense is there in returning him to prison now?"

Glattke answered: "If we do not return this man, no matter how exemplary his life may have been, we will have every man in this place going over the walls or walking away from the farm. Every man in here thinks that if he could just get out he would go straight. The simple fact is that most men who leave this reformatory return either here or to some other prison."

A third way to get out of prison is to serve the sentence, no matter how long it is. To give a perhaps exaggerated example, suppose you were sentenced to five to ten years in prison. Absolutely incorrigible in prison and unwilling to bend to authority or routine, you are constantly disciplined and you accumulate not one second of good time. You are determined to murder someone when you are released, and the prison officials know of this resolve. Because of your conduct, you serve not the five, but the ten years. But when those ten years are up, the prison gates open, you are free, and there is no legal way that you can be held any longer.

In truth, this is a potent example, for it is precisely this fear that leads judges and juries to impose long sentences on men who have committed violent or heinous crimes. The public fears such happenings—they do happen, however rarely—and the laws on the books and the sentences handed down are the result. Men who might have been reformed during a short stay in prison are sentenced to long terms and are embittered because of the hysteria such examples provoke.

Most men do not serve their full sentences. They adjust to prison, behave there, do anything and everything to indicate they have "learned their lesson" and been reformed. They accumulate "good time" and are released after serving six years and eight months of a ten-year sentence.

The fourth way to get out of prison is by parole. The federal and state governments, which operate prisons (as against jails), have a parole board comprised of expert and interested citizens. The board meets regularly at the various prisons. Members review the criminal records of the inmate, examine reports made about him by the prison staff, investigate his record in prison, and interview the man personally. The board's aim is to find those men who have been reformed in prison and to reward them by releasing them early, so that they can resume their lives. During the remainder of his sentence, the parolee is supervised by a parole officer who is supposed to help him lead a crime-free life.

Although in theory this principle is good, in practice there is a great deal wrong with the parole system. All fifty states and the federal government have some type of parole system, but there is great variance in the procedures and effectiveness of them. In thirty-nine states, the parole-board members are appointed by the governor. The other states have members chosen by state officials, the corrections agency, or have boards consisting of *ex officio* members, such as the governor and other officials. A recent study revealed that half the states had full-time boards, while twenty-three states had part-time boards, and two states had a combination of the two. In many states, the board members are political appointees who resign when a new governor is elected. In only a few instances are the boards composed of people with expertise in penology, corrections, law, and psychology.

This is not to say that many parole-board members are not dedicated. But they have an extraordinarily difficult job, trying to select those men who have sincerely been reformed in prison and who seem likely to "make it" on the outside. The board members are under such pressure because if they guess wrong and a parolee commits a heinous crime, the parole system is criticized. If they guess wrong again, they may be keeping in prison a truly reformed man who may become embittered because he was turned down for parole. The situation is especially difficult because the board reviews so many cases and has so little time in which to do so.

The parole process has been reduced largely to routine, if only because no board of men, no matter how wise, can constantly wrestle with the human factors involved in deciding who is reformed and who is not.

Some years ago I interviewed an exconvict who wished to complain about the parole system in Maryland. His description:

You can't even be considered for parole until you've served one-third of your sentence. You live for that day. You are sincerely repentant. You want to show that in any way you can. You do everything the prison asks and more. You are desperate to prove how you've changed. Then the great day comes and you go before the parole board. They ask you questions about your attitudes. You do your best to tell them how you feel. The board seems impressed. They say your prison record has been excellent. Then they say, "Keep up the good work and we'll reconsider your case next year."

You return to your cell disappointed, but you are determined to make it the next time. You try harder. A year passes and you go again before the board. They are impressed with your record. You are doing fine. Keep it up and maybe next year.

You go through this a third time, maybe, but sooner or later you give up and say the hell with it. What does it get you? You turn bitter. Nobody cares. You decide that when you get out you'll find a way to beat the system.

This man believes paroles ought to be given much earlier than they are.

It is true that parole boards almost always turn down an inmate at his first hearing. It is also true that boards are unfair, paroling one man, keeping another in prison, when their records and circumstances are nearly identical.

Such practices are in large measure the result of the system. Parole boards, with few exceptions, depend upon rather scanty information about the prisoner. The staff workers of prisons are, as we have seen, overworked, undertrained, and inexperienced. The staff is generally ill-informed about what is going on in the prison, yet they prepare reports on the pris-

oner that are crucial in the parole decision. As the Commission on Law Enforcement put it:

This information is often fitted into a highly stereotyped for-
mat. Frequently, the sameness of reporting style and jargon makes
it very difficult for board members to understand the individual
aspects of a given case and assess them wisely. This can lead to
decisions which are arbitrary and unfair as well as undesirable
from a correctional standpoint.

The basic problem is that no one connected with corrections has the slightest notion of which man will make good on
the outside.

When I was in Mansfield, I wrote a series of articles based
on interviews with selected inmates. My aim was to show how
they got into the reformatory and their attitudes there. One
young man who had been convicted of a series of armed robberies had become highly religious in prison, serving as assistant to a prison chaplain. This clergyman had given the highest possible recommendation of the prisoner to the parole
board. "If there is one man in this prison who has been reformed," he said, "it is this man." Superintendent Glattke was
dubious. He was not impressed with the inmate and flatly predicted he would be back in. Then he said:

Anyone who has been in this line of work very long learns
that there is nothing more foolish than predicting who will make it
on the outside. I've had boys I was absolutely certain were ready
to go straight. I'd have predicted my life on it. Back they came.
There were others I thought didn't have a prayer of making good.
But they did. There is absolutely no way to tell.

Arthur Glattke was one of the most respected wardens in the nation. Against his wishes, he had been appointed chief of corrections of Ohio, simply because he was the ablest penologist in the state. He resigned from that post as soon as he could and returned to Mansfield, where he felt he could be more effective working with younger men in the reformatory. His views are not to be taken lightly.

To be paroled a man must have a place to live and a job, which are enormous hurdles to surmount, for he can hardly go apartment or job hunting while behind bars. He must depend upon family or friends or overworked social workers to do these things for him. There are practical difficulties as well. He is often required by parole officers to return to the place he lived when he entered prison, although he may no longer know anyone there and his family may not welcome him. As a known exconvict, he may face social stigma, which will only make his adjustment more difficult than it is. Jobs may be scarce in that area. Indeed, paroles become increasingly difficult to obtain in times of high unemployment, such as the nation experienced in the early 1970's. There are at this writing thousands of "paroled" inmates still in prison, desperately hoping someone will find them a job so they can get out.

Perhaps the biggest indictment of the parole system lies in a sentence from the report of the Commission on Law Enforcement which states, "Actually prisoners serve as much time in confinement in jurisdictions where parole is widely used as in those where it is not."

The commission said that "no consistent or significant" relationship exists between parole and the average time served for felonies prior to release. In simpler language, this means that the prisoner would be paroled at about the same time as he would be released by serving "good time"—two-thirds of his sentence. Moreover, the person who is being released, whether for parole or good time, goes through about the same prerelease procedure. In the federal and several state systems, the person released on good time is treated as though he were on parole.

Prerelease procedures vary, but there are several common practices. An effort is made to prepare the person for return to the community. This may go on over a period of time. If his prison record is good and the staff feels he has the correct attitudes, he may be moved from maximum to minimum security cells. This will afford him more freedom to move about and access to recreation rooms and other facilities. He mingles more with other inmates and spends fewer lonely hours locked in his cell.

He may be given work that is more responsible, perhaps in the prison offices. Eventually, he will be permitted to work outside the walls, tending lawns and gardens, working the farm, repairing equipment. In such activities he is guarded and supervised much less. Eventually, he may reach trusty status, which means he is allowed to take trips into town for supplies, perhaps to work off the prison property, and even to take charge of the work detail of other prisoners.

This change in status of the prisoner is aimed primarily at helping him learn responsibility, earn trust, and adjust to his eventual release. It also helps the institution get its work done and lessens the problems of custody.

As time for release approaches, the prisoner endeavors to find a job and a place to stay. He writes to family and friends and contacts employment agencies. Counselors and social workers employed by the prison assist him. Eventually, whether by parole or by the simple passage of time, he is returned to society.

Then what happens? A description comes from Mel Rivers, an exconvict living in New York. When he got out of prison he applied for a barber's license, only to be "informed by the state that they do not issue licenses to felons. So therefore the training I had in prison was of no value to me." He went on:

I started making rounds for jobs, and found that the government agencies didn't hire ex-convicts, that places where there was a company policy didn't hire convicts. The only jobs open to me were like porter jobs, dishwasher jobs, doorman jobs—if I didn't have the keys to apartments.

Rivers said there was one occupation he knew that did not require a reference—crime. He went back to pushing marijuana and cocaine and fencing stolen goods.

Another New York exconvict, Kenny Jackson (quoted earlier), said he came out on parole at age nineteen with the usual "State-O suit and State-O-20." This is prison jargon for a plain gray suit, twenty dollars, and a bus ticket to New York, the nearest big city to the prison. When the gates opened to him, he was taken by prison car to the bus depot. As he left the car, the driver called out to him, "So long for now."

Jackson continued, "I had only one fear—fear that now you had to make good on all the talk you'd given yourself in the yard all those years, and that dreams weren't going to come true."

He started looking for jobs, knocking on doors, having them slammed "before they were hardly opened." He stayed off narcotics but began drinking to forget his problems, "and got worse on drink than I did on narcotics. I became a vicious, rotten person, no longer taking rejection." He got a gun, started pointing it at people, taking their money, drinking up their money, and landed back in jail facing a possible thirty-year sentence for robbery.

"Because one man cared for me"—an official of Alcoholics Anonymous who persuaded the judge to allow the rehabilitative process to begin under A.A. auspices—he received a suspended sentence. He sought a job working as a driver for his father's trucking business, but because he was an exconvict, it took more than eight years for him to obtain a driver's license.

Both Rivers and Jackson eventually became active in the Fortune Society, an organization of exconvicts that attempts to help other exconvicts make it on the outside and to convince young people not to become involved in crime. Both men made the remarks quoted above during talks at New York area high schools.

What they describe are anything but isolated instances.

I paid my way through college by working during the summers in factories. One summer I rode to and from work with a man from the small village where I lived. We became friends and much to my surprise he told me he was an exconvict. He had been the manager of a bank. He admitted "borrowing" some money from the bank. It was only a small amount and he was repaying it. But bank examiners found a large shortage. My friend's appropriations were quickly discovered and he was charged with stealing the entire amount. He insisted that someone else also had to be stealing, but the bank examiners refused to believe that. Never had they heard of two people stealing from the same bank at the same time.

My friend went to prison, serving five years, and his family underwent terrible hardship. His children developed emotional problems and he, an educated man—an accountant by profession—was doing menial factory work. As convicts go he was probably lucky.

More recently, I talked to a man in his early twenties. He, too, had grown up in a small town. A brilliant future lay before him. He was an excellent student, president of the senior class, a leader in many student activities. His girlfriend was the daughter of a local politician. But he began to experiment with drugs, some pot, a lot of LSD and before long he was dependent on them.

Then, to the whole town's surprise, he was arrested by the police and sentenced to prison by a judge who was determined to make an "example" of him. His sentence was cruel, one to ten years which meant he could serve as little as one but as long as ten, depending upon the parole board. It also meant he would have to serve a lot of years on parole.

He was in prison almost three years before he was paroled, an embittered exconvict not yet old enough to vote. When he returned to his hometown, nothing worked for him. His exgirlfriend's father and all who knew him were determined to continue his punishment. He could not seem to stay out of trouble, and his parole officer ordered him arrested. But he fled arrest, eventually reaching Europe, where he leads a respectable life, married to an American woman and the father of one child. He makes a living at leathercraft, a trade he learned in prison. But he cannot go home. He is a permanent exile.

These stories are not meant to provoke pity for poor exconvicts. Hardly any of them want it. They did wrong and they are willing to accept punishment. What they want was expressed by William Healy—absolution. They want forgiveness. How long must the punishment continue after years in prison? Why not give them a chance? Must society, in some sort of nonsensical pattern, force them back into crime?

Society does make life hard for the exconvict, but not all the blame can be placed there. The parole system is also at fault. President Nixon is among the many who cite the statistic that perhaps 40 percent of the men released from prison are returned there. But it is also a fact that three-quarters or more of those men are returned as parole violators.

As this indicates, violating parole is rather easy, for the parolee is forced to live under a set of rules that govern no one else in society. An adult can do just about what he wants within reasonable limits. If he is angry at his employer, he can quit the job—after "telling him off," of course—and either get a new job or be without one for as long as he can afford it. If he wants to move to another place, he can do so. If he feels like taking a trip, he can. On occasion he drinks too much. He gets tipsy, perhaps even drunk. He has a fight with a neighbor, maybe coming to blows. His circle of acquaintances may include a few unsavory types, a drunk, an addict, maybe somebody in the rackets, an exconvict or two. On occasion he might visit a few disreputable clubs or bars, place a few sporting bets, associate with a few unsavory characters. None of this will send him to prison.

Most parolees can do none of these things. Every single act in the above paragraph can—and has—put a parolee back in prison as a parole violator. A parolee and often a man simply released for good time is expected to be virtuous

indeed. He is expected to have a steady job and a regular resi-
dence and wholesome associations. He cannot go anywhere
outside of a restricted area without permission. He is granted
few mistakes and excesses. Hanging over his head constantly
is the threat that he will be returned to prison as a parole violator.

This exaggerated purity might make some sense as training the exoffender for a return to society if the parole system
were administered adequately—let alone well—but it is not.
There are about three thousand parole officers for more than
a quarter million adult felons. The parole officers are not
evenly divided. Many of them are "supervising" more than
one hundred parolees. Two-thirds of them have caseloads of
over sixty individuals. The president's Commission on Law
Enforcement gave this example of what results from such caseloads:

A parole officer feels that a 29-year-old man, on parole after
serving three years for burglary, is heading for trouble. He frequently is absent from his job and there is a report of his hanging
around a bar which has a bad reputation. The parole officer thinks
that now is a critical time to straighten things out—before it is too
late. He makes a couple of calls to find his man, without success,
then considers going out to look for him. But he decides against it.
He is already far behind in dictating "revocations" on parolees
who have failed and are being returned to prison.

There are excellent parole officers. There are parolees
who have been helped by such officers. But this is not the
norm. Most parolees get only cursory attention, showing up
for monthly reports on their activities. If they are lucky, they

get a fifteen-minute interview in which to discuss their problems. If they get into trouble with police—and police are always conscious of parolees in their district—they are returned to prison.

It is a futile, self-defeating system if there ever was one.

6 Juveniles and Jails

What happens to a youthful offender entrapped in the corrections system is best described by a lyric from an old popular song: "What a difference a day makes."

If you commit a crime and are of an age to be considered a juvenile—sixteen or eighteen depending upon the laws of the state where the crime was committed—you will become involved in the juvenile court and corrections system. This is by all accounts the best in the United States, which is *not* to say there is not a great deal wrong with it.

But if you are one day over sixteen or eighteen, you will most likely be put in jail, which is the absolutely worst part of our system of "corrections." One day, the day on which you commit a crime, can change your entire life.

A man of my acquaintance tells a story of his boyhood. The summer he was twelve, he suddenly became a delinquent. He lived in a small village in the Midwest, the sort of place that reformers have long considered the "ideal" place in which to grow up. That summer he suddenly became enamored of stealing, lying, and assorted other vices. As he tells it:

The source of my thievery was Mr. Martin's store, the rear door of which was reached through a vacant lot which lay beside my parents' house. My mother would send me to buy a loaf of bread or other foodstuffs. I went several times a day and soon had the run of the place. I'd pick out what I was to buy, write out the charge slip which my parents paid semi-monthly. It was not necessary to bother Mr. Martin at all.

The summer I was 12, I began to steal from Mr. Martin. It was so easy. While picking up a loaf of bread, I'd put some candy, pastries or cigarettes in my pocket. He never noticed. I was all hung up on cigarettes. I used to go down to Mr. Jackson's barn and smoke. I'd try every brand. I was an expert on cigarettes, not to mention cigars. Hacking and coughing, I'd light up. Later, in horror, I realized it was a miracle I hadn't burned down Mr. Jackson's barn, which was filled with hay.

One day I was stealing a pipe, which I had never tried before. I reached up and lifted a corncob pipe from a rack above the rear door and put it in my pocket. Then, as I turned around, I saw Mr. Martin looking straight at me. He said not a word. Terrified, I bolted out the door.

A little later, I improved on my thievery. My mother was treasurer of the church Sunday School. The coins brought by the children ended up in a drawer of the bureau in the dining room of my home. Later they were counted and banked. But for a few days they were an inexhaustible source of nickels and quarters with which to buy ice cream. Then I learned that my father had a habit of hanging up his pants with money in them. That was a veritable gold mine.

No one ever said anything, not my mother, not Mr. Martin. After a few months, my desire to steal and smoke went away as mysteriously as it had come. I lost interest in it and went on to something else, although I was conscious, at age 13, that I did not want to be the sort of person who stole.

Years later I talked with my mother about all this. She said she knew about it. Mr. Martin had spoken to her. The school had reported that I was cashing dollar bills to buy candy—and in those days 12-year-old boys just didn't have access to dollar bills. My mother said she was terribly worried about me, but decided to say nothing. She said she was about to step in and do something when I stopped.

I have always been grateful. I have always wondered what might have happened had Mr. Martin called the police, hauled me into juvenile court. How would my life have been changed had I been placed on probation or sent to a training school. More importantly, I've often wondered how many boys, doing essentially the same things for basically the same nonsensical reasons, have become involved in the treadmill of police, courts and corrections.

There is probably not an adult, including police officers, juvenile judges, teachers, ministers, and probation officers, who could not tell a similar story. Because a certain amount of waywardness is as natural to a child as drawing breath, reformers created the juvenile court system.

The basic principle behind it is that the juvenile offender should not be punished, in the same sense as an adult. He should not be branded a criminal but, instead, should be "corrected." Means should be found to cope with him as an individual, through a good "talking to," closer parental supervision, psychological care, and, if all else fails, removal to a juvenile institution where he can be "trained" in the proper way of life. Reformers have long recognized that it is extremely difficult to reform the experienced criminal, and that most criminals start young; therefore it is essential that the young offender be corrected before he gets into more serious trouble.

Every state, city, and county has a juvenile corrections system separate from the one for adults. Police forces have juvenile officers who work exclusively with the young. There is a separate juvenile court system. Traditionally, the youthful offender is brought before a judge, who hears the case in secret. He listens to the reports of police and social workers who have investigated the case and works out suitable corrective action with the offender and his family. Putting the boy on probation is a common result. Psychiatric treatment may be ordered.

The probation system for juveniles is normally entirely separate from the probation and parole system for adults. If some sort of institutionalization is deemed necessary for the offender, he or she is sent to a training school or reformatory. If his home is not suitable, he may be sent to live with a "foster" family.

Americans have long spent proportionately more money on corrections for juveniles than for adults. There are more juvenile probation officers than there are adult parole officers, and they have smaller case loads and thus more time to work with individual offenders. Training schools (or whatever they may be called) are more like schools than prisons. There is an absence of bars. Inmates attend classes, live in dormitories or even cottages, and have ready access to guidance.

All of this is not as good as it might be. There is need for more and better police, judges, probation officers, and personnel in juvenile institutions. There is a chronic need for more foster parents. Some institutions are overcrowded, a few are corrupt or otherwise mismanaged. Despite the deficiencies, America's efforts to correct juveniles are the best that exist. But improvements are needed.

The plain fact is that juvenile crime has been increasing at an alarming rate in the United States for many years. The system, therefore, is somehow a failure, both in deterring crime and in correcting offenders.

The reasons for this failure are a bit of a puzzle. Increased population and urbanization may be part of the reason. Return a moment to Mr. Martin of the story told earlier. In that small Midwestern village, he could perhaps have supported one boy's juvenile depredations. He knew him and his family. He could speak to him or to his parents. But if every boy in town had been stealing from him, or if his store had been in a city where scores of children, none of whom he knew, were stealing, he would have had no recourse but to call the police. A few, whom he caught, would be turned over to authorities. Surely, some of this goes on. And how many storekeepers are as considerate as Mr. Martin was?

More importantly, it is undoubtedly hopeless to ask even the most model corrections system to make up for the failures of home and society. Juvenile offenders come from a wide variety of circumstances. Some come from affluent homes where there is plenty of money and a stable family life. Others come

from the ghetto, perhaps from a broken home with only one
or even no parent. The juvenile offender may grow up in a
subculture where crime and illicit conduct is a badge of
honor; or, in a middle-class home where the aberrations of his
parents lead to psychological problems. He may come from a
seemingly "ideal" home and the reasons for his waywardness
appear to be unexplainable.

But there is perhaps a more tangible reason for the failure
of the juvenile system—that single day when the person is no
longer a juvenile offender. Whether it is his first offense or a
prolongation of his juvenile misconduct, the day he becomes
involved in the adult system—pity him.

If he is lucky, he will commit a felony and go to the reformatory or penitentiary for adults. As horrible as they are,
these adult institutions are models of perfection when compared to jails—and it is to jails that most young misdemean-
ants go, whether to await trial or to serve out their sentences.

As already stated, no one knows what goes on in jails. It
was not until 1970 that the federal government even got
around to *counting* how many jails exist—over 4,000. By all
accounts they are dreadful places. In addition to being old,
many are overcrowded, with two, three, and four people in a
space designed for one. More than a few jails even lack modern toilet facilities. At best they have only minimal educational, recreational, and religious facilities, and often these
consist of just a television set or a radio or a space in which to
walk around. Prisoners are simply *kept,* herded together without classification. The jails are dens of homosexuality, violence, and corruption in which simple survival is often an
achievement. No effort at correction is made at all. Parole
and probation is unusual for jail inmates. To be sent to an

American jail is a one-way ticket to doom. It is only remarkable that some survive the experience and emerge to lead productive lives. That fact is a testimony to the best in the human
spirit.

Harvey Swados, writing in the *New York Times Magazine*
in April 1970, reported the following quote from a twenty-
one-year-old Puerto Rican who had just been released from
the New York City "reformatory" on Rikers Island.

Man, I was so lonesome. That was the worst part of it. I
didn't have one friend. I had two terrific teachers there, Lucas and
Goldstein, when I was getting my high-school equivalency certifi-
cate, but I couldn't talk to them about what was bugging me. It
would have been breaking the rules. Aside from them there was
nobody I could trust. Nobody. Not even the guy in the cell with
me. Because if they got something on my roommate, how did I
know he wouldn't try to hang it on me?

You always had to be tough. That was the big thing, to be
tough. I didn't *feel* tough, but I couldn't let on. Even when the
guys would take off [sexually assault] somebody, it would turn
my stomach sick, but I'd have to be one of the leaders or get
marked chicken. What I'd do, I'd help to make the guy give in,
then when it came my turn I'd say, "Ah, the hell with it," and I'd
head for my cell. Night after night after night, I'd lay there
masturbating—that was all there was for me.

Then I'm out. All of a sudden, bang, I'm standing on Queens-
boro Plaza, and I say to myself, "Is this what I was waiting for?"
I go back to my street and to the apartment, and everything looks
so small, not like I thought about it in the reformatory. I lay down
in my room and I say to myself, "Well, here it is, the same old
crap." And I can't stop thinking about the way they were always
counting you, over and over, like animals. Or the Puerto Rican
guy that committed suicide. I really liked him, but after he cut up

[slashed his wrists], the guard that got him the razor blade laughed and said, "Well, that's one less." I cried myself to sleep that night. I really don't know why I didn't cut up myself. Or hang up.

And this institution may be one of the best in the nation. This young man at least went to school while in jail.

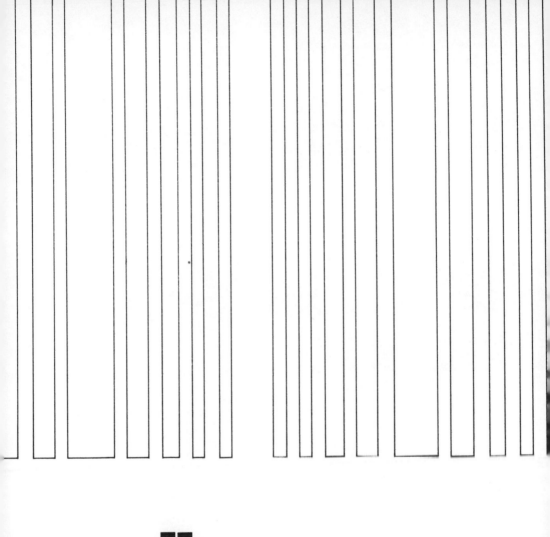

PART II The Solutions

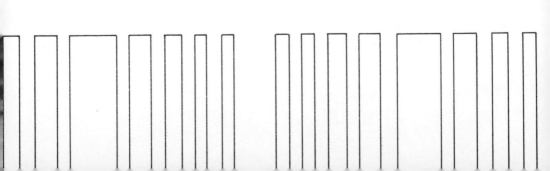

7 A New Set of Laws

Many solutions have been offered to America's prison problem. The suggestions range from building more and bigger prisons with higher walls to tearing them down altogether. Some people feel the United States must spend billions of dollars to construct a new penal system. Others have said this is unnecessary; we have at our disposal the means and know-how to establish an effective corrections system, if we only had the will to do what we know how to.

An issue that fascinates reformers is whether crime and violence are *innate* in man. In his provocative book, *The Crime of Punishment,* Dr. Karl Menninger, a famous psychiatrist, suggests that human beings *want* crime. We *need* it. When a crime is committed and the offender is caught and punished the guilt feelings of everyone are somehow assuaged. We all have the seeds of violence and criminality in us and we act them out in the misadventures of others. Dr. Menninger writes:

We disown violence, ascribing the love of it to other people. But the facts speak for themselves. We do love violence, all of us, and we all feel secretly guilty for it, which is another clue to public resistance to crime control reform.

What is it about violence that so intrigues us? Is it man's true nature? Are we all so violent, so destructive, so criminal at heart? Is it an "instinct"?

Yes! There can be no doubt of this fact in spite of the occasional waves of pollyannism and denial.

Dr. Menninger cites as evidence our long-standing national preoccupation with crime. We buy millions of detective and murder mysteries every year. Even young children play "cops and robbers." More biographies have been written about such famous bandits as John Dillinger and Jesse James than about many of our presidents. Crime and the apprehension of criminals is an important theme of movies, television, and the theater. Every newspaper reports crime stories, and in the event of a major crime, its coverage may take precedence over all other news of the world. We are indeed fascinated by crime.

Dr. Menninger further argues that our innate, animalistic nature demands vengeance as a form of punishment. Because all of us are "guilty," we wish to see the criminal caught and punished as a means of absolving ourselves from our own fantasies and our guilt about them.

Maybe. If Dr. Menninger is correct in saying that we do not solve the prison problem because we do not *want* to solve it and need it to fulfill an inherent human need, then we might as well all give up. A person might be able to reform a prison, but how can one reform human nature?

Fortunately Dr. Menninger argues with himself, perhaps unwittingly. He mentions that in the past the sick and injured were objects of public shame and embarrassment and that hospitals were bestial places hidden from public view. Today this has changed to the point where hospitals are objects of community pride in nearly every city and town and are visited regularly by the public. He mentions a similar change in attitude toward the mentally ill, who are no longer chained in dungeons but are instead viewed as sick, sent to a hospital for treatment, visited by family and friends, and released into society when they are considered well. He might also have mentioned similar changes in attitudes toward the mentally retarded, blind, deaf, and other handicapped people.

At some time in the recent past, it might have been argued that sickness, physical affliction, and mental illness fulfilled an innate human need, assuaging guilt, so therefore these people had to be hidden away and mistreated. It certainly can be argued that public attitudes changed not because we shed our collective guilt, but rather because we came to realize how vulnerable each of us is to such afflictions and sought and discovered improved techniques of treatment and retraining.

Dr. Menninger makes the highly appealing point that the prisons, which seek to treat the afflicted and deficient in our society, ought to be as open and as much a matter of civic pride as the hospitals, and the schools for the deaf, blind, and handicapped. Why don't we visit the prison where the wayward in our society are being treated? Why don't we open up our arms and welcome back into our midst the criminal released from prison as we do a person who recovered from a serious illness or operation?

In answer, a person can speak of inherent, irrevocable guilt feelings. But there is at least one other possible answer: we know that jails and prisons are bad and do not reform anyone. To carry on the medical analogy, we welcome the former tuberculosis patient back into society, because we know the hospitals are good, and he has been cured. If we believed he was likely to continue to infect everyone he met, our attitude and behavior would be different. Society simply has no confidence that the criminal has been reformed.

There is evidence to support the contention that Americans want prisons and prisoners reformed. In 1969, the Joint Commission on Correctional Manpower and Training employed Louis Harris and Associates to poll public opinion relative to prisons and prison reform. Here are Harris's major findings:

- The American public is aroused over the growing crime in the nation, with 89 percent of Americans believing that crime has increased in the areas where they live.

- Six in ten adults believe our system of law enforcement fails to discourage people from committing crime.

- Only 51 percent of adults believe the prison system has done a good job in helping to cope with the crime problem.

- While 48 percent of the adults believe that rehabilitation is the major focus of prisons today, 72 percent believe that it *should be* the main emphasis.

- Similarly, while 24 percent feel that the main purpose

of prisons today is the protection of society, only 12 percent believe this should be the main emphasis in the future.

• Only 7 percent of adults believe that the purpose of prisons is to punish offenders.

• Only 5 percent believe that prisons have been "very successful" in rehabilitating criminals.

Clearly, "innate" feelings or no, Americans want a better correctional system. If the Harris poll is correct, it is equally clear that the American people are, as they have been so often in the past on other issues, far ahead of the experts and elected leaders whom they have entrusted with the power to deal with these matters.

Perhaps the most startling finding of the Harris poll is that only 7 percent of adults believe the purpose of prisons is to punish. The plain fact, however, is that 100 percent of the nation's criminal laws have that purpose. This is a starting point for reform.

American criminal law is still based on "an eye for an eye" philosophy—it seeks to punish. If you rob a bank, it will cost you ten years of your life in prison; steal a car and be punished with five years in prison; peddle narcotics and it will cost you thirty years; plan and execute a murder and you will either be murdered yourself or spend the rest of your natural life in prison. Punishment, punishment, punishment. Law upon law calls for it.

The justification for this is "deterrence." As initially stated in Chapter One, this means we will not do something because we know we will be punished for doing it. We are all enamored of deterrence. Simple common sense, the life experience of most everyone, tells us that deterrence is a big factor in human conduct. In the rearview mirror of our automobile we see a police car. Automatically, we check the speedometer, slow down, and become perfect drivers. When the police car turns off the road, we sigh with relief and speed up. Clearly, if more police cars were in sight the accident rate could be greatly lowered. It has been proved many times.

There is an item in the store that appeals to us. How nice to have it. It would be so easy to "heist" it, stick it in our purse or pocket. But we do not. Someone might be watching us. Suppose we were caught. Think of the embarrassment— arrest, publicity, the judge, fines, even jail.

How much of an effect, however, does deterrence have on crime? Every motorist knows the penalties for drunken driving. He may even believe that drunken driving is such a serious offense that the penalties ought to be increased so the person who drinks is simply unable to drive. Yet more than a few motorists do drink and drive. Why aren't they deterred?

A normally law abiding citizen, driven to the brink by a combination of circumstances, flies into a rage and beats his wife, his children, a friend or neighbor. Did the thought of punishment deter him? Hardly.

Strangely, there are still people who believe in punishment as a deterrent to crime. Richard G. Kleindienst, deputy attorney general of the United States in the Nixon administration, the nation's second highest law enforcement post, said in 1970:

The crime rate will . . . be reduced when sentencing practices once again reflect the object of deterrence as well as the objective of rehabilitation. When a potential offender believes he will "get off easy" if he is caught, he will not be deterred from committing a crime.

Maybe. But study upon study by psychiatrists and psychologists, the entire futility of our laws, the self-defeatism of prisons indicate that few people, certainly among the young, consciously and callously set out to commit a crime because they are unaware of the penalties. They *know,* but they are not deterred. There are surely many reasons why crimes are committed—and probably no one knows all of them: anger, folly, belief one will not be caught, impulse, guilt feelings, a momentary don't-give-a-damn attitude, stupidity. But the sum total of all the reasons is that fear of punishment does not deter the criminal. It may in fact goad him into crime so he will be punished.

All of this gets us into that never-never land of psychology and psychiatry. To have a good system of corrections we need to know a great deal more about why people commit crimes and what goes on in the mind of the criminal. But there is a lot known now that is not used. In the last half century, the behavioral sciences have developed abundant—perhaps overwhelming—evidence that punishment is much less effective in controlling conduct than is reward. A person will act in anticipation of a reward far quicker and easier than he will if he is beaten half to death. Mental institutions and a wide variety of schools have practiced such techniques for decades to good effect. American education stopped rapping the recalcitrant student on the knuckles a hundred years ago and began passing out gold stars and "A's." Our criminal laws still call for rapping criminals on the knuckles—and a whole lot worse.

Consider the problem of the American judge. Before him stands a young man convicted of a crime. The offender has brains and talent. He could be useful to himself and to society. The judge wants to help him. How can he do it under the law he is sworn to uphold? Probation? The judge knows that probation officers are overworked. Besides, it has been tried already and it has not worked, for here is the offender before the court again. Prison? The law book tells the judge that the crime committed by the offender carries a penalty, generally stated as a minimum and a maximum sentence, of "X" number of years. But whether for one year or twenty, the judge knows he is sending the offender to a pesthole where he is not only unlikely to be reformed but will in all probability be made worse. He is not reforming the offender. He is ruining him. What is the judge to do?

Frantic efforts have been made by some judges to come up with alternatives to prison. Youthful offenders are sometimes put to work repairing the damage they did to a victim or working for him until they have repaid the money they stole. A number of young men have been given a choice of the military service or jail. Not too long ago, a judge gave a young woman who had desecrated the American flag the choice between jail or marching through town carrying a flag. She marched. Another alternative is to sentence a person to employment, which would supply workers for the endless list of tasks that must be done in hospitals, mental institutions, churches, playgrounds. Streets must be swept, parks cleaned, flowers planted. In addition, exconvicts could be put to work helping parolees and other exconvicts to obtain jobs, places to live, and to adjust to freedom.

The point is that Americans must rethink and rewrite our criminal laws. They are hundreds of years old in many cases, the product of old thinking that is discredited today. England, from which our laws stem, has reformed its penal system. A prison sentence of more than five years is rare in Britain and occurs only in cases of particularly heinous crimes involving incorrigible individuals. The death penalty has been abolished. In the United States, five years in prison is considered a "slap on the wrist," handed out for minor crimes against property. Routinely, judges impose sentences of ten and twenty years and longer.

The ultimate sentence in the United States remains the death penalty. There is, however, mounting evidence that it may not be with us much longer.

The death penalty—sentencing a man or woman to death by hanging, electrocution, or gassing—has long been controversial in America. Its proponents argue that it is necessary as a deterrent. They argue that a man will not commit a murder if he knows he will die for it. Simply looking at the daily newspaper indicates that the deterrent does not work. Murders are committed, death penalty or no. In fact, the death penalty may be an invitation to murder by those deranged souls who wish to die out of a gross sense of guilt. What more noteworthy death can there be for them than to be executed for murder? The opponents of the death penalty argue that the "eye for an eye" attitude no longer fits modern man, that murder is murder whether committed legally by the government or illegally by the individual, that in the execution of an offender, man is admitting his failure. Society is saying, "We cannot reform you, for we do not know how; therefore, you must die."

The argument over the death penalty has been going on for decades. Several states, led by Michigan, have already outlawed executions, and many state governors, acting under their powers in states where the death penalty persists, have routinely commuted death penalties to life imprisonment. Now the issue is before the United States Supreme Court. The opponents of the death penalty are arguing that executions are a "cruel and unusual punishment," which the Constitution forbids. The high court has said it will hear and hopefully decide the issue. It has already overturned the sentences of thirty-nine men because the jurors who convicted and sentenced them were selected because they were known to be unopposed to the death penalty.

Because of the Supreme Court test and the fact that each person on "Death Row" is given every possible opportunity to appeal his conviction and sentence—as well as the public outcry against executions—no person has been executed in the United States since 1967. Meanwhile, the courts have continued to sentence people to the ultimate punishment. When Charles Manson and his accomplices were sentenced to death, they became the six hundred twenty-first, second, third, and fourth people awaiting death. They made ninety-nine people in line for the California gas chamber. Florida is second with seventy-two. As Anthony Lewis of the *New York Times* observed, "How curious it is that the Sunshine States should head this grizzly list." *

There are people who have been on Death Row for years —and Death Row is a special place, perhaps a form of inhuman punishment itself. Condemned men and women do not mingle with other prisoners. They live in the most maximum of security cells, under close guard, for the state does not want these people to cheat the executioner by committing suicide. No effort is made to rehabilitate them. They are condemned, after all. They spend nearly all their time in their solitary cells. Only a brief period of exercise is permitted.

---

* These statements antedate the California Supreme Court decision in February, 1972, to abolish capital punishment in the state.

One of the problems of penology has been to find a "painless" way to execute people. The French came up with the guillotine, a large knife that plunges down to chop off the head. Although no one has ever described the experience, it is or was considered a "humane" way to kill people. Contrary to public belief, immolation is also supposed to be a painless way to go. Pouring gasoline on oneself and striking a match may be repulsive to the onlooker, but the immolator supposedly dies instantly.

Some years ago, when I was a reporter there, Maryland changed its mode of execution from hanging, long considered one of the least humane ways to eliminate people, to gassing. A bright new gas chamber was installed at considerable public expense and a reporter was assigned to witness its first use. The reporter returned a shaken man. The prisoner had been placed in the gas chamber, the door locked. The cyanide pellets were dropped and the chamber filled with gas which was supposed to execute the man within seconds.

Something went wrong. He coughed for half an hour.

Six hundred and twenty-four people await death. That is a lot of people. It is larger than an army battalion. They could not all fit into most movie theaters in the United States. It would be half the population of the Ohio village in which I grew up. Chances are it would equal the entire enrollment of the school you attend. Imagine the public outcry if the entire population of your school died suddenly.

To start killing all these people now would create a national bloodbath of unprecedented proportions. It is unthinkable that the American people would stand for such mass killing, legal or not. This is the foremost reason why the death penalty may not be with us too much longer.

8 Reforming the Courts and Police

There can be little prison reform unless the police and courts are also reformed, for they comprise a triumvirate. Police, courts, and corrections go together like the angles of a triangle, our three branches of government, the three legs that give the crudest milkstool stability.

Among the many who have recognized the corrections problem as three-pronged is Ramsey Clark, former United States attorney general, who stated:

Merely to add more police, or increase the district attorney's staff or provide additional judges, or build a new jail will not be enough unless that happens to be the single deficiency of the system within that jurisdiction. There is no such jurisdiction.

New York City is an illustration. Reacting to public dismay over crime in the streets, the city beefed up its police force to over thirty-two thousand men and women. This gigantic force (there are only eight thousand FBI agents!) is well-trained and well-equipped. As police forces go, New York's is efficient in arresting offenders. The result has been a most serious overloading of the city's criminal court system and jails. There are long delays in trials at which justice is haphazard at best. Jails are filled to two and three times their capacity. Many of the inmates are simply awaiting trials at which they may be acquitted.

Fortunately, a great effort is underway to improve the nation's criminal courts. Leadership has been assumed by Chief Justice Warren E. Burger. In many speeches, articles, and interviews, he has appealed for reform and goaded lawyers, judges, and legislators into action. He has begun to make an annual "State of the Judiciary" report.

Court reform would be relatively simple if all that were needed were more and bigger courthouses and the appointment of additional judges and prosecutors. These are needed, but the best legal minds in the country recognize that much more is required. There is today widespread recognition that the centuries-old system might have worked splendidly when the United States had a population of four million, but that it is creaking and breaking down under the weight of two hundred million people.

The deficiencies of the court system and the ideas for improving them form too large a subject for this book. But some of the major points relative to corrections can be described briefly.

● There is great need either to shorten or speed the process of determining the guilt or innocence of a person. In major crimes years can elapse between a man's arrest and his either going to jail or being released as innocent. Mohammed Ali, the former heavyweight boxing champion, waited four years and spent a reported $250,000 on appeals before the United States Supreme Court declared him innocent of draft evasion charges. It is not at all unusual for a person, tried and convicted, to appeal through the various levels of the state courts, then take the appeal to the federal courts. No one is suggesting that the appeals process be eliminated. It is vital protection against a person being wrongly convicted. But legal scholars are seeking ways to speed the process, if only by the addition of more appellate courts and judges.

• Some courts have already taken steps to eliminate the postponements that plague the lower courts. One method is to have the same judge follow the case through to its completion. This way he would be aware of the delays sought by the defense. Another method is to require the defense to pay the court costs for every day a trial is postponed.

• Great effort is being made to improve the nation's bail system to reduce the number of people in jails awaiting trial. All too often the amount of bail required for release prior to trial is just an arbitrary figure arrived at for no apparent reason. A bail of from five hundred to five thousand may be set for the same crime. Many judges are now attempting to standardize the bails and to make them much lower, as well as to eliminate them entirely in many cases. A noteworthy contribution has been made by the Vera Society in New York City through which law students interview people who are in jail because they are too poor to afford bail. Recommendations are made to judges to reduce bails or to release the person on trust. The law students then follow through to see that the person appears for his trial. This effort needs to be greatly expanded around the country.

• Our "adversary" trial system is being seriously challenged. In this system the prosecutor and the defense attorney battle each other. They argue over court rules governing the admission of evidence, the forms of questioning, the procedures of the trial. The trial is delayed by "motions" for the judge to decide. These are meant to lure the judge into an error so the decision in the case can perhaps be reversed on appeal. The American trial is often a "circus" in which the question of guilt or innocence becomes lost in legal technicalities. Many of the important facts in the case are simply never made known. This is not the only way to conduct trials. Some European trials are more like a hearing before a judge who makes every effort to bring forth all the pertinent facts so that guilt or innocence may be truly decided.

• Attempts are underway to improve the quality of judges and lawyers in the criminal courts. Criminal law has long been the poor relation of the legal profession. With precious few exceptions, the ablest graduates of law schools have gone into corporate or some other form of the law that is more prestigious and higher paying. For the most part, the practice of criminal law has been left to the inexperienced, less able, and more unscrupulous. Assistant prosecutors, even when able, are usually young and view their job as a stepping stone to a political career.

The result has been a sea of troubles. There are "defense" lawyers who prey upon poor families who are ignorant of the law. One common racket is for a lawyer to approach the family of an arrested person and offer—through his "connections"

—to get the sentence reduced. He does, however claim he needs several hundred dollars to "pay off" the prosecutor. The family goes into debt, at times for years, to raise the "bribe." The lawyer pockets the money, then engages in the normal process of plea bargaining with the prosecutor. The lawyer cannot lose. He pockets a big "fee" and the family thinks he is marvelous because the prison sentence was shortened. The racket is not uncommon even though the legal profession has been trying to end it for years.

The Supreme Court has ruled that every defendant must be represented by a lawyer. If he cannot afford to employ one, the court will appoint one for him. There is a severe shortage of such lawyers, especially competent ones. Suggestions have been made for larger payments by courts or other forms of subsidy to attract more and better-qualified lawyers for the defense.

Similarly, there is need both for more criminal court judges and for better ones more deserving of the respect lavished upon them in the community. Most judges are hardworking and dedicated, but there are some who are not. One complaint is that judges and prosecutors work only a half-day on the job, while complaining of "overcrowded dockets." Nor is the conduct of judges always judicial. In July 1971, a committee of the American Bar Association drafted a policy that calls for a judge to "suppress his personal predilections and control his temper and emotions," as well as to avoid "repartee" and "unnecessary disparagement of persons or issues." In his book, *Crisis in the Courts,* Howard James estimated that half of the 3,700 state trial court judges were "for one reason or another unfit to sit on the bench."

Reforming the court system will be difficult and take

many years, but this reform is probably more advanced than that of the police. The nation's foremost legal minds are actively seeking solutions and bringing great prestige to programs to carry them out.

Police reform is usually expressed in terms of more and better-qualified policemen, improved equipment and training, higher salaries. All this is needed. But a great deal more is required if the vital police function in corrections is to be fulfilled.

Policemen today lament the loss of their image as the protector of society, the keeper of order. Gone, along with buggy whips and bustles, apparently, is the image of the friendly, neighborhood cop, walking his beat, patting children on the head, and straightening out wayward boys with a little man-to-man chat. This still happens far more than most people believe. But, the image of the policeman today is all too often that of an enraged man in a riot helmet, swinging a nightstick and throwing canisters of tear gas, charging into demonstrators of various racial and political persuasions. The image of the wise, fatherly protector has given way to that of the bigoted sadist. This is surely regrettable.

To a certain extent the policeman is not at fault. There are few reports of the good he does. No television camera zooms in as he saves a life at the risk of his own. He still talks to misguided youngsters and tries to help them as best he can, but no reporter is there, pen in hand, to record the conversation. When he delivers a baby, foils a robbery, settles a family quarrel, takes a lost child home, there just is not very much "news value" in it.

But a certain amount of the policeman's loss of image is his own collective fault. He also too often forgets to be impartial and he is paying a price for that today. The policeman, individually and collectively, has always been the one to decide which laws should be enforced. The books are full of laws that are never enforced. The policeman has always made such decisions as whether he sees a crime, which one was committed, and how vigorously he wants to do something about it.

The policeman is being haunted by some decisions of the recent past. He chose to see crime during the civil rights demonstrations of the early 1960's and often charged in with clubs, water hoses, and whips. He saw crime in demonstrations on college campuses and raced in to stop it. There are many who will defend his actions, perhaps correctly, but the policeman's image is largely derived from his actions in seeking to suppress dissent that he did not personally like. Greater impartiality and restraint could have prevented that, as police have shown many times.

The police may not have been racially prejudiced, but they have looked like it until quite recently. The attacks upon peaceful demonstrators is only part of the evidence. Include the shortage of black policemen, the failure to promote the ones that there are in rank, the arrogance and use of racial epithets by white policemen in black neighborhoods, the less energetic investigation of crimes against black people.

The best police forces in the nation have adopted reforms to correct these abuses. Policemen are learning to be more impartial, at least when demonstrations are peaceful, and to show more restraint when they are not. Most departments have energetic programs to improve relations with racial and other minorities. But it must be said the reforms still have a long way to go.

Part of the police problem in corrections is that the policeman receives "good marks" and promotion on the basis of arrests and crimes "cleared." He has a reflex action to prevent crime by making an arrest. The result is an overloading of the courts, jails, and prisons. Perhaps there is something to be said for police receiving "good marks," too, when they save a person by failing to arrest him, take him home, send him to a church, hospital, or other agency that can help him.

Police do such things on a more or less regular basis. To suggest that such measures would greatly reduce the crime rate is ridiculous. At their very best, police are struggling against a "crime syndrome" in which lawlessness is at least sometimes condoned and honored. To ask the police to cope with all the resultant crime is to ask too much. In a democracy only those laws can be enforced that the people want enforced. The police truly need help in the form of more effective courts and corrections, just as the latter two need more effective police.

But surely there must be a better way to solve the crime problem than by pecking away at it with arrests and tossing the arrested into jails where they are more likely to be worsened than reformed.

9 In Search of Prison Reform

The nation's leading penologists and corrections officials gathered in Philadelphia. There was a natural division among them. Some, called the "old guard," wanted to continue the stern, punitive measures that they believed would rehabilitate offenders. The reformers wanted new, improved methods to make corrections more humane and effective.

They argued for days. The reformers won. The convention became inspired with zeal for reform. In the end, the convention adopted thirty-three principles that would guide prison reform in the United States. The major ones were:

No. 4—"The best legal and psychiatric knowledge should be employed" to differentiate the "mentally sick" from the "criminally responsible."

No. 9—Repeated short sentences imposed for recurring misdemeanors or petty offense are ineffective, both as a means of correction and as a punitive deterrent.

No. 10—"The architecture and construction of penal and correction institutions should be functionally related to the programs to be carried on in them."

No. 12—Correctional workers need "special professional education and training of a high standard . . ."

No. 13—The goal of rehabilitation will be best achieved by individualized treatment of the offender.

No. 14—The offender should be sentenced on the basis of "full consideration of the social and personality factors of the . . . individual."

No. 16—The prisoner should receive the "generally accepted standards of decent living and decent human relations. Their food, clothing and shelter should not be allowed to fall below the generally accepted standards . . ."

No. 18—"Rewards for conformance to the highest values of our culture should be given precedence over fear of punishment in guiding the development of human character in correctional systems . . ."

No. 19—"No law, procedure or system of correction should deprive any offender of the hope and the possibility of his ultimate return to full, responsible membership in society."

No. 20—"Moral forces, organized persuasion and scientific treatment should be relied upon in the control and management of offenders, with as little dependence upon physical force as possible."

No. 22—Every effort should be made to raise the educational and vocational skills of offenders.

No. 23—"To hold employable offenders in correctional

institutions without the opportunity to engage in productive work is to violate one of the essential objectives of rehabilitation."

No. 24—Psychiatric services should be provided to those offenders and prisoners who are abnormal.

No. 27—Suitable employment for a discharged offender is a "major factor" in his rehabilitation and the "regaining of his lost position in society."

No. 29—With few exceptions offenders should be released under parole supervision.

No. 33—"The correctional process has as its aim the reincorporation of the offender into the society as a normal citizen. . . . Constructive community contacts should be encouraged. The success of the correctional process . . . can be greatly enhanced by energetic, resourceful and organized citizen participation."

Enlightened principles surely.

Who can quarrel with them?

The convention that drafted these principles of prison reform was held in the year *1870!*

Today, over one hundred years later, these principles are still the *goal* of corrections officials. Observance of the principles is more an exception than a rule. Dr. Menninger described the men who drafted the principles:

Can anyone read these amazingly intelligent, high-minded, far-visioned principles without a surge of admiration for the humanity and the intelligence of our long dead predecessors, and a sigh of regret for the dismal contrast of present practice with these noble ideals?

Remember, please, that these men had none of the modern inventions or conveniences. They knew nothing of indepth psychology, dynamic psychiatry, behavioral sciences, or social case work. Given no decent facilities or equipment for reforming men, they kept their charges in the gloomy dungeons and bleak castles considered appropriate at the time, and employed untrained, illiterate help to guard their wards.

But they had their ideals and their principles and they had come to envision better things. They were men and women who had been hired by the state to treat rough men roughly, to make them sorry, and to keep them miserable. Nonetheless, they erected and proclaimed a higher conception of their job. Untrammeled by the wretchedness of their appointments and the vindictiveness and unenlightenment of their tax-paying supporters, they met and formulated their purposes and their methods at a level that would be ultramodern in any institution today—one hundred years later. . . .

Reformation of the individual is *still* not the purpose of our system. The infliction of vindictive suffering has *still* not been repudiated. The prisoner *still* has little to do with his destiny, and can scarcely imagine that he does have. Prison discipline, far from gaining anyone's good will or conserving anyone's self-respect, *still* tends to do just the opposite. And a prison whose primary aim is to make offenders into "industrious, free men rather than orderly and obedient prisoners" is yet to be born!

Can the reader think of any other human discipline—any science, any art, any industry, any department of our civilized life— which, in this past hundred years of turbulent expansion, has made so little progress in bringing practice up to ideal and vision?

Today's penologists, wardens, and administrators of corrections want these principles put into practice as much as their predecessors did a hundred years ago. Perhaps to a man they do their best to carry them out despite horrendous difficulties and limited resources.

The modern corrections official is thwarted by the prisons themselves. The monstrous buildings were erected of stone and steel as fortresses to keep criminals in custody. The buildings were built exceedingly well and seemingly indestructible. They remain useless in reforming prisoners, but eminently usable to punish them. There are not a few who believe that prison reform might begin with the systematic destruction of most prisons, replacing them with housing projects, parks, playgrounds—or, better, more useful tools of correction.

Lack of money stands in the way of penal reform. State and local governments are chronically strapped for funds, at a time when citizens are demanding more and better governmental services. What politician is going to siphon off funds that might be used to assist law-abiding citizens and voters to give aid and comfort to the social misfits in prison? Only the certain knowledge, recently accepted, that the products of prisons prey upon society has led to a change in this thinking.

The chronic lack of funds for prisons has left a terrible legacy. There are jails in the United States where a prisoner is fed on sixty cents a day. Salaries paid to prison personnel are among the lowest in the nation. A recent study showed that two-thirds of the "line workers," such as guards and other personnel dealing directly with inmates, of juvenile institutions earned less than $6,000 a year. More than a third of such workers in adult institutions were in these pay brackets. Only a rare individual earns more than $8,000 a year. Indeed, 30 percent of the *supervisors* in juvenile institutions earn less than $6,000 and almost half the supervisors in the adult field earn less than $8,000.

Such pay scales hardly attract qualified, capable men and women. In fact, the typical prison guard is an older man who has failed in another line of work. He takes the job for security. More than a few have mental and emotional problems not unlike those of the prisoners under their charge.

Any sort of prison reform demands more money for higher salaries to attract and keep competent correctional personnel—at all levels—wardens, doctors, psychologists, social workers, supervisors, and guards.

Until the last few years, no American college or university trained individuals for work in corrections. Prisons had to make do with whomever they could find to fill a job and hope he would learn on the job. Today a few universities—hardly enough—are preparing students to enter correctional work.

But more than higher salaries and better preparation is needed. A public-opinion survey showed that corrections ranked last among thirteen leading occupations in its appeal to teenagers. Clearly, there is need to upgrade corrections as a profession, giving it more of the status offered the businessman, scientist, teacher, lawyer, or doctor. Even the much-maligned policeman has more status than the corrections officer, at least in the opinion of teenagers.

The personnel problems of correctional institutions are difficult, but they are not without suggestions for solutions. Ways must be found to open up jails and prisons to the public. Schools, hospitals, and mental institutions have found ways to make use of a variety of volunteer assistance from the community. It is a century past time that prisons did so.

If jails and prisons could be made less closed, less secretive, less offensively brutal, a variety of assistance could come from the community. Clergymen have long been volunteers in prisons. There are many others who would help, doctors, former nurses, exteachers, ordinary people to work in the kitchen or commissary an hour a week, talk with prisoners, do favors for them, offer some kindness and politeness in contrast to the brutality of prison life.

Industry offers a vast, largely untapped source of vocational training. Many businesses would be willing, a few eager, to provide equipment and personnel to train convicts as potential employees. Such programs exist in vocational high schools and urban ghettos. They are instituted partly out of altruism, but mostly to obtain good employees for the future. If prison programs were presented properly to industry, there is reason to believe they would be accepted.

Exconvicts form a tremendous source of virtually untapped volunteer labor. And this is strange. Consider the success of Alcoholics Anonymous through which, in simplest terms, exdrunks help drunks defeat their problem. The same principle has been used among drug addicts and gamblers. There are thousands of exconvicts who have made it on the outside, many of whom are eager to work with convicts and parolees, to counsel and guide them so that they can also make it. Such programs are so effective precisely because the former drunk, addict, or convict knows the problems and attitudes of the sufferer better than anyone else. The Fortune Society in New York seeks to use exconvicts in this fashion, but most prison administrators have turned a deaf ear to it. Exconvicts are no more unwelcome anywhere than in their former prisons. Such attitudes are merely astounding.

Most correctional administrators would like to involve the prisons in the community. It is today the most important goal of such people. They know it must come to pass. They are hampered in part by "blind spots," such as old ideas of the need for custody, an unwillingness to invest trust in inmates or those who come in contact with them. But in the defense of correctional officials it must be said that part of the problem is that prisons are such depressing places. Many of the inmates have attitudes that would scare away the most dedicated volunteers. Worse, most prisons are located in rural areas, where community resources are limited. But, problems or no, steps must be taken in the direction of opening up the prisons.

10　Prison Reform Programs

Each prisoner is an individual. No two are alike, and therein lies much of the problem of prison reform.

The same prison may house an experienced safe-cracker who is determined to prove his skill; a sex criminal acting out his aggressions against his parents; a man of subnormal intelligence who can be taught to read and write with only the greatest difficulty; an educated, idealistic person who breaks the law as an act of dissent; an addict, trying to escape life's hardships with the needle; a product of the ghetto, whose entire way of life tells him that the people who get ahead are in the rackets, that to be law-abiding is to have a life of toil and squalor; a drunk; a man unable to contain his rage and sense of desperation—and many, many more.

There is no *one* way to reform such a diversity of human beings. There must be *many* ways—and many ways are being tried.

But the simple, ungarnished fact is that many of the efforts at reform are doomed for failure at the outset. Corrections officials are working with most imperfect tools. They are in a sense trying to build a computer with a hatchet. Put another way, modern man frequently cannot identify the problem of the criminal, let alone solve it.

At his most enlightened, today's reformer recognizes that many criminals have serious mental and emotional disturbances. Their crimes are not the products of reason or choice. They simply cannot help themselves. Therefore, prison reform would seem to call for a vast increase in the psychiatric services offered in prisons. But psychiatry is most imperfect. Repeated studies have shown that Freudian psychology, the most popular in the United States, has about the same effectiveness as no treatment at all.

There are certain disorders that psychiatrists and psychologists find particularly difficult to treat. There is no systematic knowledge of either the causes of or of the solutions to these disorders. Foremost among these is the psychopathic or sociopathic behavior. In simplest terms the psychopath or sociopath is an individual who is antisocial, frequently violently so, who *uses* people. He seems to have no conscience or sense of guilt. Paranoia, a sense of persecution that can lead to violent acting out of alleged wrongs, is another extremely difficult problem for the psychiatrist to deal with. So are homosexuality, drug addiction, and alcoholism. The simple fact is that sociopaths, paranoids, homosexuals, addicts, and alcoholics form an unknown but extremely large percentage of the populations of prisons.

None of these people are considered mentally ill. It would be extremely difficult to have them committed to mental hospitals. They are called "criminals" instead and dispatched to prison. Admittedly, they need help, but the most enlightened of prison administrators find it grossly difficult to help them.

A central fact of prison reform is that even if all was done to assist prisoners that modern man knows how to do, there would still be a large number of prisoners that no one knows how to reform. They seem to be resistant to the best efforts of corrections. About all anyone knows how to do is to keep them in custody, releasing them into society in hopes that things will not turn out too badly. There is a need for some sort of prison, detention center, or whatever it might be called. But it does not have to be a brutal, dehumanizing place.

As long as the old fortress prisons are in use, there is not a great deal to be done in the way of reform. But wardens are trying everything they can think of. A main thrust is toward permitting inmates greater choices and expressions of individuality.

Better classification of inmates is a major goal. If the inmates can be separated by the nature of their offenses, background, and chances for rehabilitation, it is believed this will make prison management easier and increase the chances for reform. The experienced criminal, the aberrated will have less chance to contaminate the person who sincerely wants to reform.

Greater efforts are being made to move prisoners from maximum to minimum security cells and into trusty status,

when it is believed they are ready for it. All this is rather difficult in the fortress prison, but the effort is being made any-
way.

Progress has also been made in relaxing the prison rules
that were developed over the years. Prisoners are permitted to
decorate their cells and move about more freely. Just having a
time in which the cells doors are unlocked and the inmates
can move about in the cell block is considered progress. They
are being given opportunities to make their own rules and to
manage aspects of prison life.

Administrators are trying to minimize the amount of
marching about and herding of prisoners. Simply putting
smaller tables in the dining hall and allowing the men to con-
verse is progress. Likewise, it is progress to allow men to
make use of the library, recreation room, or other prison facilities.

Another badly needed reform is to pay inmates higher
wages for working in the prison industries. It would be ideal if
the inmates learned skills that would be useful on the outside.
But even if they did not, they could at least earn respectable
wages for the work they do, thereby enabling them to support
their families, accumulate savings, and learn the monetary
value of regular work. Who can doubt that it would be beneficial to a prisoner to discover that he can make more money
by working than by stealing? It is a simple fact, but prisons
seldom teach it. Paying respectable wages to prisoners for
their labor would greatly increase the cost of running prisons,
but it is important to reform. It would certainly be cheaper
than the cost of keeping the families of prisoners on welfare.

Attempts are being made to permit prisoners to maintain
contacts with families and friends. The censoring of mail has

been relaxed. Visitation rights have been extended. It is quite common today for an inmate and his family to have a picnic in the prison, sometimes on the grounds. A small number of prisoners are being permitted to leave the prison for a weekend with their families as part of their prerelease program.

A few prisons are permitting wives of prisoners to pay extended visits to the institutions. A pioneer in this type of reform is the Mississippi State Penitentiary at Parchman. On the first and third Sundays of each month, inmates and their wives are allowed to be alone in small buildings scattered throughout the twenty-one-thousand-acre institution. They are able to spend several private hours together, maintaining some semblance of a normal married life. The program is credited with easing the sexual tensions, which are the scourge of prison life, and with permitting inmates to maintain their roles as husbands and fathers. California has recently adopted a similar program. In neither case are unmarried prisoners permitted conjugal visits.

Prison administrators are trying to find ways to break up the do-your-own-time subculture of prisons and to make inmates more receptive to the medical, psychological, sociological, and educational services, however limited, which the prison can offer. The method being used most often is the *indeterminate sentence*. It is now widely used in the federal system and in California. The offender is not given a fixed sentence. Rather, he is sent to prison until he can establish to the satisfaction of correctional authorities that he has reformed and can be released safely.

The desired effect of the indeterminate sentence is to do away with the "good time" philosophy. The quickest way for an inmate to get out of prison is not to mind his own business and stay out of trouble, but to participate in the correctional programs and to convince administrators that he has been re-habilitated. One barometer of the effectiveness of such sentences is that prisoners do not like them. It is far easier simply to put in time, stay out of trouble, maintain an aloofness from the correctional staff, and keep peace with fellow prisoners than it is to make a sincere effort to correct oneself by regular visits to the psychologist, sociologist, counselor, or teacher. The indeterminate sentence is considered essential to reform. Its use seems likely to increase.

But even the best efforts in the fortress prisons are only stopgap. Since the buildings themselves make rehabilitation difficult, the main thrust of prison reform is to find ways to put inmates in smaller, more homelike institutions from which they can become involved in the community.

There have been several efforts at such reform. One of the oldest is the "minimum-security" prison. Gone are the high stone walls, the guard towers, the armed men patrolling the in-mates. At the most there will be a chain-link fence with a gate. Sometimes there is no fence at all. The inmates live in buildings similar to college dormitories or, at worst, to army barracks. In spite of its appearance, such a building is still a prison. The windows are made of shatterproof glass and are constructed in small panes, as in Cape Cod houses. The ribs of the windows are made of unbreakable steel. And the doors have pickproof locks.

The inmates live in rooms, perhaps with a roommate or two. They have the freedom of the building, which includes a television set and other recreational facilities. A counselor is present. The inmates make many of their own rules. During the day they work—often on a farm—or attend school. Such institutions are considered a million times better than the fortress prisons.

Another type of institution, used frequently with young offenders, is the "cottage" type institution, which has no security at all. It is simply a small building housing a dozen or score of inmates, although the structure may be located on the grounds of a "training school" or "reformatory." A "house mother" or "house father," perhaps a couple, is in charge, seeking to treat the inmates in a kindly, parental fashion. The inmates go to school or carry out other assigned tasks. There is considerable freedom of movement. Such institutions are a vast improvement in juvenile corrections.

Efforts have been made to carry this even further. The young offender is not sentenced to a juvenile institution at all. Indeed, he may not even be sentenced. The judge simply "arranges" for him or her to spend a period of time at a "home" operated by a religious or charitable organization. A rather small group of young people live and eat in the home. They have total freedom to come and go and do as they please. The men and women running the home do not feel that they are involved in corrections. They are not operating a prison or reformatory, but a home where boys and girls live. Each person is treated individually and with kindness and respect. Every effort is made to meet their needs and to help them surmount their problems. Such programs have been very effective with young people in trouble.

The most recent and celebrated of such techniques are the "halfway houses," which the Federal Bureau of Prisons opened in 1961 in New York, Chicago, and Los Angeles. The name stemmed from the original concept that the men being prepared for release from prison were "halfway" out of prison. Later, judges began to sentence men to such institutions, so they were said to be "halfway" into prison. Several states have since adopted the program. It is considered the apex of prison reform.

A halfway house handles about twenty prisoners. Some occupy a large single-family dwelling. Others occupy scattered rooms in a YMCA hotel. All are located in the community. Access to public transportation is essential.

The occupant (the term *inmate* is inappropriate somehow and *convict* would never be used) wears civilian clothing. He generally arrives at the halfway house by public transportation, without escort. For a day or two he is restricted to the building, although he may receive visitors. He eats in the house dining room or, if in a YMCA, in the public cafeteria. After a day or two of orientation and counseling, the occupant goes out to look for a job. Once he finds a job, the occupant is gradually given more extensive leaves for recreational purposes and for family visits. As his parole or release date approaches, he will be permitted to move out of the halfway house, returning for conferences on a regular basis.

Halfway houses are staffed by regular prison personnel, who are highly trained in counseling. One full-time staff member will be an expert in employment counseling. College students studying the behavioral sciences may be employed on a part-time basis. Emphasis is on individual counseling and group therapy. Probation officers attend these sessions, particularly as the occupant nears release.

Such counseling is considered highly beneficial, since counselors are not working with difficulties of the past or imagined ones of the future, as in prison, but with the day-to-day problems of the occupants. Misbehavior by residents of halfway houses is common, particularly among youthful offenders. Drunkenness, fights, auto accidents, tardiness in returning to the institution, unsavory associations occur, although perhaps a majority of occupants do not have such difficulties. The advantage of the halfway house is that counselors are able to detect the problem immediately and work intensively with the offender. If he does not respond to counseling, the offender can be returned to prison or the counselor can recommend a delay in parole until conduct improves.

Everyone in corrections knows that halfway houses, homes, cottages, and minimum-security prisons work in a high percentage of cases, if the institution is run well and the offenders are carefully selected on the basis of adaptability to such programs. The problem is that there are not nearly enough of them. Such centers are rather expensive to maintain when compared to the cost of running a regular prison. To handle hundreds of thousands of people in this fashion would take an immense amount of money. An additional problem is that halfway houses are not welcomed in every neighborhood: the Harris poll showed that most people approved of halfway houses in principle, but did not want them in *their* neighborhood.

Everyone interested in corrections knows that ways must be found to involve offenders in community life. Locking up the criminal and throwing away the key simply has not been the solution. If the offender can work and live in the community, while being counseled to surmount his problems, he can be prepared for full participation in society. Emphasis today is on a vast increase in community institutions. Short of this, prison administrators are seeking to use the limited facilities available to maximum benefit by moving prisoners as rapidly as possible from the fortress to minimum-security institutions to halfway houses.

Failing in this, prison administrators would like to see a vast increase in work-release programs in which inmates live in the prison but spend their days working outside. Their earnings defray the cost of their imprisonment and support their families. This program was first tried in North Carolina, where there was great fear that released inmates would prey on the community. But with few exceptions it did not happen. In North Carolina, as well as in many other places where it has been tried, it has been highly successful.

Another important approach to prison reform is simply to reduce the number of people in jails and prisons. The thinking is that a large portion of the people behind bars have no business being there. If these people were taken out, the jails and prisons would be left with the truly criminal and misguided. With their task thereby simplified, administrators could then concentrate upon genuine reform.

An estimated third of the people behind bars may not need to be there. It has been maintained for decades that drunks and addicts, whose crimes are a product of their habit or addiction, should be placed in situations that are designed to help them break that habit or addiction—not in jails or prisons.

The mentally disturbed and retarded are others who do not belong in prison. But most courts are encumbered with a legal definition of insanity—generally the ability to know right from wrong—that has no relationship to the emotional disorders of the offender. He may have known he was doing wrong, but could not help himself. Sending him to prison—the best of prisons—creates a burden on administrators. They simply are not equipped to provide the intensive psychiatric care the offender needs. All the prison can do is worsen his condition.

The prisons also contain large numbers of people who should reasonably be out on probation or parole. As their counterparts of a century ago believed, today's corrections officers feel that probation and parole will work effectively if given the means to do so.

In simplest terms, the United States needs more and better probation and parole officers and procedures. The personnel of parole boards must be improved and their procedures streamlined so that they can better judge which prisoner should be paroled. More and better trained help is needed to accomplish this task.

A large increase in the number of probation and parole officers is clearly dictated. Experiments have shown that when the case load of these officers is reduced to more workable limits, say thirty individuals, they are much more effective in helping offenders stay out of prison. The officers are thus able to provide the time, attention, guidance, and practical help needed. Lightened case loads also provide time to innovate new programs.

11 The Last Word

The United States has many problems. Implementing solutions for most of them will take a lot of money. The cost of correcting the nation's urban problems, perhaps foremost among our ills, has been estimated at one *trillion* dollars. Improving the nation's standard of health will cost a great deal of money, as will improving public transportation. Ending the pollution of air and water will cost gigantic sums in one form or another.

One of the refreshing things about prison reform is that, as such things go, the price tag will not be very high. The court system could be improved for relatively little money. At the present the United States spends about $128 million a year for its federal court system—less than half the cost of one large military transport plane. Simply doubling the expenditure could work wonders.

No one is advocating great expenditures for new jails and prisons. Some are needed, to be sure, but no responsible person is recommending the erection of new fortresses of stone and steel. Greatest expenditures will be needed for more and better corrections officials. But we are not talking about gigantic expenditures that are beyond the powers of taxpayers to comprehend.

What we need most is a little money and a lot of will. Indeed, if much of the money currently spent were *better* spent, we would have gone a long way toward reform.

We need, more than money, changes in attitude toward crime, criminals, punishment, and reformation of offenders. I do not personally believe that the American people have an innate need for crime and punishment. Rather, I believe they need leadership and guidance to develop, recognize, and carry out those programs that will end the futility, self-defeatism, and waste of our corrections system. This leadership can come only from elected officials and from professional administrators of the corrections system.

There is much heartening evidence that such leadership is coming at last. The statements of President Nixon, congressional hearings, the formation of the Law Enforcement Administration to channel funds into improving the corrections system, the appointment of many government study groups, the utterances of leading judges and scholars, the committees formed by the American Bar Association and other groups to recommend changes—these and many other developments point to a climate of reform.

All such efforts and more that should come need support —from you. They need a citizenry that realizes the folly of our existing system, insists upon changes, and endorses those programs likely to improve it. With the eighteen-year-old vote now a fact of American life, young Americans have an unparalleled opportunity to do something at last. Prison reform is one problem you *can* do something about.

Reading List

American Correctional Association. *Manual of Correctional Standards*. 5th ed. Washington, D.C.: The American Correctional Association, 1969.

Barnes, Harry Elmer. *The Repression of Crime*. New York: George H. Doran Co., 1926.

Barnes, Harry Elmer, and Teeter, Negley K. *New Horizons in Criminology*. Englewood Cliffs, N.J.: Prentice-Hall, 1951.

Cleaver, Eldridge. *Soul on Ice*. New York: McGraw-Hill, 1968.

Gillin, John Lewis. *Criminology and Penology*. New York: P. Appleton-Century, 1935.

Jackson, George. *Soledad Brother: The Prison Letters of George Jackson*. New York: Coward McCann, 1970.

Knight, Etheridge. *Black Voices from Prison*. New York: The Pathfinder Press, 1970.

Malcolm X. *Autobiography of Malcolm X*. New York: Grove Press, 1964.

Menninger, Karl, M. D. *The Crime of Punishment*. New York: The Viking Press, 1969.

Sands, Bill. *My Shadow Ran Fast*. Englewood Cliffs, N.J.: Prentice-Hall, 1964.

Index

About the Author

Robert A. Liston was born in Youngstown, Ohio. He received an A.B. from Hiram College, Hiram, Ohio, where he majored in history and political science. He began his writing career by working for magazines, but in 1964, he became a full-time free-lancer. He is the author of about twenty books. Among his most important books for young adults are: *Tides of Justice* (Delacorte); *Greeting: You Are Hereby Ordered for Induction* (McGraw-Hill); and *Downtown* (Delacorte), which was selected by *School Library Journal* as one of the best books for young people published in 1968. *The Edge of Madness* is Mr. Liston's second book for Franklin Watts. His first was *The Limits of Defiance: Strikes, Rights, and Government.*